VIOLIN DOWN

Interior design: Marc Whitaker / MTWdesign.net
Back Cover Author Photo: Larey McDaniel
Back cover photo: Weller Hall

Printed in the United States of America

Violin Down

John Weller

FOREWORD BY IRA LIEBERMAN

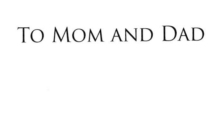

TO MOM AND DAD

CONTENTS

FOREWORD

When people think of violin virtuosi, they may picture talented individuals, sensitive to musical stimuli, trained by gifted teachers, practicing for long hours in the confinement of small rooms, then judged strictly by conservatory faculties. Through the entire process their confidence grows with burgeoning technique and musical prowess. As a reward from the gods, they receive a career performing before an adoring public. Nothing has hindered their ascent of Valhalla.

This proved not to be the path of the young virtuoso John Weller. Initially his progress on the violin was almost magical, as if preordained. It was devastatingly interrupted. After disappointing attempts to continue, John had to accept the probability that he would never play again.

This is the compelling story of John's coming to terms with the loss of his life's ambition and the lengthy process of reclaiming his art. He speaks honestly about preparing for a future without the violin, the strength of character he found in himself, and the people who helped him begin his arduous return journey.

John's account of that journey, filled with emotional detail and sketches of friends, colleagues, teachers and mentors, will strike chords of recognition in every artist.

In fact, readers of John's story will find themselves curious about the background stories that hide behind the professional façade of every musician.

Dreams are the food of all artists. John discovered the courage to trust his own imagination to lead him to different dreams. His inspiring story encourages us to surprise ourselves and, in so doing, discover our own new strengths and dreams.

Ira Lieberman, *violinist, is a member of the First Violin Section of the Metropolitan Opera Orchestra and the New York Pops Orchestra at Carnegie Hall. He holds the BA, MA and PhD degrees from Columbia University. He and John Weller became colleagues and friends as members of Lincoln Center's Mostly Mozart Festival Orchestra, playing with the world's top soloists.*

Beyond earthly rewards, creating sound artistically becomes a musician's life force, the reason even to draw breath. A worst nightmare is to be denied this primal oxygen, that of expression through the vibrations of musical beauty. Any musician who has fallen under the spell understands, and dreads, the spiritual devastation that lies one small step away from the joy of making music.

This is an account of a lifelong love affair with the violin. But it is also a tale of catastrophe, a plunge into an abyss of the deepest despair and loathing for the violin.

This is the true story of a tremendous fall from grace, of a young man who lost the gift of music through a catastrophic event, his lifelong effort to recapture his passion, and the scars of a struggle that remain etched forever.

Present Day

My eyes are almost blinded by the bright stage lights as I squint into the audience. I'm not looking for anyone in particular. I'm just trying to get my bearings. On stage with me to my left is the entire Seattle Symphony Orchestra and to my right a packed concert hall. There is a violin and bow in my hands, and I'm wearing a set of tails, white tie and black patent leather shoes. I have done this a thousand times, but a sweaty wave of dread is washing through me as the house lights begin to dim. My mind won't let it go, and I'm panicking once again, *what the hell am I doing here?*

In the printed program my name is titled "Assistant Concertmaster" which seems to indicate I know something about playing the violin, how to make the bow go back and forth, and how to play the notes up and down the fingerboard. The violin does feel familiar, but a force is pulling me back in time, back into a horrific nightmare. My shoulders stiffen as my thoughts dredge back to the events of so many years ago. I grasp my violin tightly to know it's still there, and grip my bow so that it doesn't drop to the floor.

Somehow I am able to exorcise the dark power that possesses me, and rejoin my fellow musicians in the present moment. The audience is applauding the entrance of the conductor and I try to join with the smiling faces as we all settle in to begin the concert.

The panic passes for the most part as the music swells, and I try to relax into the rapture of playing some of the world's greatest music. My heart pulses with the music's rhythm, but it also pounds with the deep fulfillment I feel playing the violin in a great symphony orchestra. I cherish each note with vibrato and sing through every phrase as if it's the last music I'll ever play.

There was a time in fact that I had played my last note.

It's impossible that I'm on this stage. It's impossible that I'm playing the violin at all.

Spring 1975

It was around noon, and just outside the Portland State cafeteria, when a vaguely familiar face appeared out of the crowd: *"John is that you! How's violin?"*

The question stabbed into my heart painfully and I couldn't help but cringe. I had hoped never again to hear such words. I had hoped never again to cross paths with anyone who might inquire about what had happened to me.

It was Tom, a fellow I barely remembered from high school, but who unfortunately clearly remembered me.

He had apparently admired from afar my meteoric rise with the violin throughout our years together at Adams High, but had lost track of me after graduation.

"Hi Tom, really good to see you again," I lied.

"I guess there's no way you could have known," I said. "It feels like it's been a long time."

"I quit violin over two years ago."

1

There is a very beautiful old building on the campus of Concordia College in Seward, Nebraska. It's named after the school's founding president, J. George Weller, my great-grandfather. Weller Hall is also where another George Weller, my Dad, taught music, German and theology after graduating in 1949 from Concordia Seminary in St. Louis, Missouri. Dad was already an accomplished organist, and upon graduation from seminary became an ordained Lutheran minister as well.

Newlyweds in Nebraska

In 1950, Dad married a former student of his, Norma Rose Koch, a stunning beauty from Worthington, Minnesota. Mom probably felt out of place in the wilds of Nebraska, but Dad's philosophical depth, academic prowess and passion for music had won her heart.

After my older brother Paul was born in 1951, Mom and Dad moved to St. Paul, Nebraska, some 60 miles to the west. Dad was installed as the pastor of two churches, one in St. Paul and the other thirty miles away in Loup City. He held these positions for three years, and it was there in St. Paul that I was born in 1954. I don't remember anything about the place though, because we all moved to Portland, Oregon when I was ten days old.

Portland, 1954: Dad, Paul, John and Mom

Dad had taken on a professorship at the Concordia College in Portland, and also performed the duties of organist and choir director in the chapel. Playing the organ was Dad's first love, but his greatest passion was choral direction. Eventually his Concordia choir was touring as far away as Montana. Mom ran the household as those earliest years in Portland rolled by, and in 1957, my family increased to five when my younger sister, Carol, was born.

By 1960, a large new church had been built just down the street from the college. From the small and charming chapel at Concordia,

Dad moved into the spacious organ loft at St. Michael's Lutheran, becoming its first organist and choir director. Dad now worked at both Concordia and St. Michael's, which were linked, not only in proximity but in Lutheran theology and shared personnel.

Our house was about five blocks from Concordia, where Paul, Carol and I grew up under Mom's strict edict of *"Erst die Arbeit!"* "First the work!" (THEN the play). School and household chores seemed to consume so much of our lives, but I got away with what I could, building forts in the yard, and go-carts that always crashed dramatically in the alley. I climbed trees to the top branches and "swam" on the tops of hedges in the neighborhood, oblivious to the scratches and bloody knees every other kid on the block had, too. My brother, sister and I reveled in that innocent time, in an innocent neighborhood, among innocent friends.

As much as we played with abandon outside our house, there was something extraordinary going on inside at the same time; something that colored each living day with emotion and depth. The poignant melodies of Bach's St. Mathew Passion, Beethoven's *Pastoral* symphony, Dvorak's Cello Concerto, Tchaikovsky's *Nutcracker Suite*, the violin concertos of Bruch and Mendelsohnn, Humperdinck's *Hansel and Gretel Suite*, Haydn, Beetho-

Sharing a moment of melancholy with Carol

ven and Schubert piano trios, early music from the time of Praetorius and much more; this music drifted throughout the house and accompanied every moment of our lives. Mom and Dad always had music playing, serenading us from the record player.

Half the time we were probably unaware that this powerful music was coursing through our subconscious and pulling on heartstrings we didn't even know we had. But this music became a part of each of us, and we recognized the timeless and crushing beauty of it together as a family over the years. Along with the liturgical and choral music we listened to weekly at St. Michael's, Mom and Dad were teaching us to love the world's greatest music.

On Sunday mornings, Dad always left early to play the first service at St. Michael's and the rest of us would arrive later in the morning for the second service. We often heard Dad playing as we entered the church, and the power of the mighty pipe organ would shake my emotions almost physically. By the time I was seven or eight, I liked being up in the organ loft during services where I could be with Dad, watch his hands fly over the keys, and skip his feet confidently over the pedals below.

As a son, I felt proud watching Dad lead the congregation through the hymns and liturgy, often with no music in front of him. The large congregation seemed to take comfort in his musical leadership. They were there to worship, but they were also an audience. Dad performed, and they responded and sang with passion. I sensed the respect and warmth that flowed Dad's way as a man of music.

Dad invariably launched into a stirring postlude as the congregation rose to exit the church, and this was always my favorite part of the service. I would get myself ready because I knew it was coming, the last chord of the piece; the culminating victorious fortissimo where Dad's left foot would find that lowest possible note and hold onto it forever. I wondered why music affected me like that. I would just burst, then turn to cover my face so no one could see me cry.

Paul, Carol and I took piano lessons from Mom in those years. Mom was quite a pianist herself and also enjoyed leading the children's choir at St. Michael's. In college she took art classes, and could sculpt and draw with great sensitivity. Mom saw that we all took ballet too – like it or not – because she loved dancing and movement. Dad installed two sets of ballet bars in the dining room with hand railings he found from an old demolished hotel, and he also rescued a large framed mirror that completed Mom's dance studio. I didn't care for piano or ballet. I would whine and protest at every piano lesson, as there were always friends outside waiting to play, and dancing just wasn't for me. Mom enrolled us at a studio in the Hollywood district for ballet lessons conducted in the Russian style. I never could get those arm and hand gestures to look quite graceful enough, and those tights, sagging between my knees with each *plié* . . . pure humiliation! Our strict ballet master, Ivan Novikov, tapped out our dance rhythms with hardwood blocks, but he also used them to whack my shoulder blades: "Dooon'd zlouuuch!"

From kindergarten on, we attended Kennedy Elementary School, which was about five blocks in the opposite direction from Concordia. I was an average student, but Paul excelled and was always on the honor rolls. Early on, he took up cello and studied privately with Maria DeRungs, who was considered the premiere cello teacher in the Portland area. Mom used her own love of dance to work a trade with Mrs. DeRungs: dancing lessons for her children in exchange for cello lessons for Paul.

Cello lesson with Maria DeRungs

Mom teaching dance

I admired Paul and tried to emulate his maturity throughout my youth. We both joined Little League baseball, which I loved, even though I seemed to strike out most of the time. I think I got on base once or twice, but only because they let me use the T-ball stand.

These were also lazy days of ambling home from school, bicycling around the block, roller-skating, and shooting basketball into the evening hours as the neighborhood dogs barked at our heels. Sometimes Dad woke Paul and me at 4:30 in the morning for fishing trips to Horseshoe Lake, where, still sleepy-eyed, we hooked our slimy worms and dreamed of perch and bluegill.

Dad had loved lake fishing since he was a boy. North of his hometown of Fort Wayne, Indiana, his father had bought a humble cottage on Lake James and this was a magical place we vacationed to regularly over the years. Our family train rides on the Great Northern route were tremendous adventures, but the lake itself took on mystical proportions. Nothing was more exciting than putting a line in the water and watching the bobber plunge, and the dynamic of a boat's bow plying the waves became a wonder to my senses for years to come.

Mom and Dad were socially progressive in thought and deed. They cared about more than our core family and demonstrated this by opening our home to those in need. We had a foster sister, Beverly, for four years and a foster brother, Allan, for two years. They added challenge and meaning to our lives, and we took them in as family for the duration of their stays with us. Allan was slightly older and bigger than me and a little on the rough side. He'd beat me up occasionally, but if I began to whimper, he would stop and we'd be friends again – until the next time! In later years, we took in an interracial infant as well. We were set on adopting Sidney outright, but his biological mother asked that he be returned to her, and we lost him forever.

In the fall of 1963, my family took off on a grand adventure. We moved to Berkeley, California for a year when Dad took a sabbatical leave from Concordia. He had received an offer that allowed us to live rent-free in exchange for taking over the organ and choral duties at a Lutheran chapel near the University of California. Dad felt it would be a gift to the family to have such an experience beyond Portland.

Our house in Berkeley was on steep Marin avenue and within the first block above the traffic circle at it's foot. Any hint of eucalyptus immediately transports me

John, Paul, Carol, foster brother Allan. 1961

back to that neighborhood where we climbed on nearby Indian Rock and explored along winding Shattuck avenue. The sunlight there was different from Portland, as was the climate and the floral growth. As foreign as this new world was to us, we embraced Berkeley as an enchanted place.

On the recommendation of Maria DeRungs, Paul was accepted as a student in Berkeley by the tremendous Margaret Rowell, arguably the most respected pedagogue of cello on the West Coast. Mrs. Rowell taught cello in a holistic and imaginative way, often using an assortment of soft rubber toys as teaching aids. Placing a small green turtle on the body of the cello, she would have Paul roll his fingers around in it, imitating precisely the gooey and organic movement of a luscious vibrato. She always wore the flowing dress of a grande dame but incongruously wore heavy and clunky shoes. Obliviously stomping on the floor, she really meant "Use more bow!", as she felt so intimately and vicariously attuned to her student.

I remember the trips to her house were an almost vertical drive up the steepest streets of Berkeley. She lived in the clouds up there at the top of the hill, another reason she took our breath away.

Paul enrolled at Garfield Junior High and Carol and I at Oxford Elementary School, which was an easy and almost magical walk from our house. The new sights and adventures at Oxford and our new friends were a daily fascination. The songs we sang and the fun we had on the playground felt like the sweetest of times.

But I will always associate the sensations of Berkeley with a defining moment in history. It is the interior of my fourth-grade classroom, and my pretty teacher's contorted face, that remain etched in my memory of a particular day. The principal had entered our room to say that school was over, to go home, that President Kennedy had been shot.

In the years before Berkeley, I had often found myself restless and melancholy. I was uncooperative, rebelling against what felt like Mom's oppressive tactics for ensuring we did our chores and attended our piano and dance lessons. Mom loved dancing so much though, that to my chagrin, ballet classes continued even in Berkeley. At Madame Sawitzka's popular studio downtown, I suffered through yet more endless barre exercises and *grand jetés* across the floor for all to see. Ballet lessons only fed that inner melancholy and I was ripe for escape.

Music itself had ached in my heart from my earliest memories, thanks to Mom and Dad. It seemed only natural to be moved by its power, but little did I really know how deeply it could be a part of me until Berkeley.

The music teacher at Oxford, Mrs. Blanc, visited our classroom and asked who wanted to play an instrument. Up shot my hand, along with a number of others. It was she who then suggested the violin to me. I had mentioned that my brother played cello, and Dad the piano and organ, so her face lit with the obvious choice: "You could play gorgeous trios together", she enticed.

Out of her quiet suggestion, I was about to discover the love of my life.

It was the first time I ever opened a violin case. Sunlight filtered in through the windows of our front room and straight onto that violin. It was only a humble rental from Oxford, but the violin glowed in front of me as if in anticipation. I felt the strangest sensation right away: never had I even seen a violin up close like this, much less touched one before. Yet, I felt that I could already play it. I knew somehow that all the music Mom and Dad had been surrounding us with would soon be within my own grasp.

I started private violin lessons right away with Gretchen Meisner, a young violinist from the Oakland Symphony, and at the same time, I joined my school orchestra at Oxford. I was off to a good start. The idea of making the notes go up and down with my fingers seemed so simple. And mistakes aside, playing in tune was such an obvious thing to do. I never went through a screeching and scratching phase because I thought "anyone knows what a violin sounds like!". Almost right away, I was playing *The Babbling Brook* and *La Cinquantaine*, accompanied by Dad at the piano.

They were doing something right, there at Oxford school. It only went up through the sixth grade, but the orchestra had full string sections. We set up in the school cafeteria where we played *Pat-a-Pan* and other simple pieces that grabbed my heart. There were the over-whelming numbers of flute and clarinet players too, but we didn't sound like a band. We sounded like an orchestra.

From the first day, I loved being a part of it. Mom said I calmed down when the violin came into my life. Violin and I had found each other, and I had taken my last ballet class.

That magical year in Berkeley ended all too soon. By the summer of 1964, we were driving our ungainly Buick with trailer in tow back to Portland. As we made our way north, we stopped in the redwood forests and points along the Oregon coast. Dad discovered a new fishing hole for us, Siltcoos Lake near Honeyman State Park. We settled into the modest resort motel there, and while Mom and Carol stayed ashore, Dad, Paul and I trolled out of the channel in a rented boat and found the sprawling lake full of perch and bass. We would return there numerous times over the years as a family tradition.

As the new school year began that fall, we began our search for a new violin teacher. Once again turning to the recommendation of Maria DeRungs, we made a connection with one of the top violinists of the Oregon Symphony, Eugene Kaza. He was also the beloved music man at Grant High School, where he directed one of Portland's major high school marching bands and had also cultivated a large and respectable classical orchestra. Taking me under his wing, he had only to point the way as I practiced through one etude book after another.

Eugene Kaza

Back in Kennedy School, fifth grade was fun and easy as I had this "thing" I did on the side now with violin. Mr. Kaza's comedic humor and Hungarian passion for music was inspiring, and within only a few months he decided that what we had accomplished on violin was worthy of some recognition. He decided that it was already time to present me in front of his high school orchestra.

2

At Grant High School's winter concert, there I stood, playing the solo violin in Vivaldi's A-minor concerto. It was January 1965

rant High
Dates Event

Eugene Kaza, director of music at Grant High School has prepared a program for Saturday, Jan. 23 at 8 p.m. in the high school auditorium which will include the debut of an 11-year-old violinist in the Vivaldi A-minor concerto.

John Weller, son of Mr. and Mrs. George Weller will play the first movement of this concerto accompanied by the Senior Orchestra. The orchestra will also play the overture to "Der Freisch by Weber and Copland ckeroo Holiday."

The Junior Band will perform a Bach chorale, a pair of marches and a fantasy on "The Wizard of Oz."

The Senior Band will be heard in works by Bach, Souza, Scriabin and Corelli as well as a suite entitled "A Night at the Ballet."

and the date just happened to fall on my eleventh birthday. All I remember now is the euphoria; the pretty girls in dresses, smiling faces, the doting attention. Violin and I had simply melted together since Berkeley. It seemed to come as naturally as my own voice

Violin continued to soar that year, and at age twelve I auditioned into the Portland Junior Symphony as its youngest member. I loved hearing my tone blend with the rest of the orchestra. Beethoven's mighty Eroica symphony was up on my first rehearsal. I sat last chair in the second violin section, just ahead of the trombones, but what a sound. What a tremendous

Trios with Dad and Paul. Wearing my Grower's Fruit Little League jersey

emotion to be a part of. Combining my own voice with the Beethoven bound me into the most intimate and timeless connection. Instinctively, I could already foresee that the violin and I were entering into a powerful mystery that extended beyond the horizon.

The Junior Symphony rehearsed twice a week at Holladay School, just west of Lloyd Center, and concerts were performed at the ornate Oriental Theater on Grand Avenue. The almighty Jacob Avshalomov conducted the orchestra, and we played his own fabulous compositions as well over the years. "Mr. A" commanded great love and respect among the young musicians, not only because of his profound passion for the music, but also for his firm patriarchal

John Weller, 13, is youngest musician in the Symphony where the average age is 16.6 years. This is John's second year.

manner. The full orchestra rehearsed on Saturday evenings, but on Wednesday nights individual string sectional rehearsals were held. Sometimes these rehearsals were difficult and intimidating to me, but mostly I fell deeply into the sensations of what it is to play great symphonic music on the violin.

Paul had won a position in the Junior Symphony as well, and for the first three years, we played in the orchestra together. Dad usually chauffeured us to rehearsals, and it became a much anticipated tradition, that on the way home after some difficult music-making, we would stop at the Broadway Dairy Queen for Dilly Bars.

For the five years that I played in the Junior Symphony, life was a blur of rehearsals and concerts, evenings of chamber music, and playing in the organ loft of the church. At St. Michael's, Dad often composed descants and accompaniments to various chorales so Paul and I could join in on cello and violin. I found playing for services deeply spiritual, if but only on a musical level. And whether from Junior Symphony, church or my own practicing, the day's melodies were always going through my head. Violin just vibrated all that music into my bones.

I was thrilled to earn my first paycheck, a fortune of $15 playing in Concordia College's production of *Bye Bye Birdie*. It was presented in the gymnasium over a number of nights and playing backup in the popular Broadway style was tremendously exciting. The show-tunes were not nearly as challenging as playing Brahms or Tchaikovsky with the Junior Symphony. By comparison it felt like child's play, which in that sense, it probably was at my age.

In the eighth grade, I was voted student body president of Kennedy School! The election meant very little in fact, except as a lesson in democracy or civics. But this was very important to my homeroom teacher Mrs. Drew. She had been politically active before her teaching career, even traveling as a state delegate to a presidential convention. Banners were painted, campaign speeches given, and the votes tabulated, so the process all seemed quite meaningful at the time.

The slogan from my own campaign poster, composed by a fellow student, proclaimed:

> Now he's no Rockefeller,
> But for Kennedy he's a seller!
> No one could be sweller,
> So vote for Weller!

Mr. Kaza saw my way in to many Oregon Symphony concerts, at which I always sat in starry-eyed anticipation. Nathan Milstein, playing Lalo's Symphonie Españole, was the first of a parade of violinists I was fortunate to hear. Mischa Elman, Isaac Stern, Ruggiero Ricci, Leonid Kogan, Sidney Harth, Henryk Szeryng and a very young Itzhak Perlman followed as the seasons passed. Mr. Kaza got me backstage where I could meet them, get their autographs, and dream of following in their footsteps.

No matter the concerto, I was already familiar with the music from our record player at home. By the time I attended a concert, I knew by ear every nuance of the Beethoven, Tchaikovsky or Sibelius concerto. Watching and listening to it in person was like living through a dream, but while still wide awake.

During Saturday morning chores I might be scrubbing the kitchen floor, but with eyes streaming tears as I blasted out Oistrakh playing the Brahms concerto on the stereo. At crucial moments in the concerto I would run, with dripping washrag, to press an ear up close to a speaker. This seemed to transport me into the live performance. The habit also helped while listening to Dad's scratchy old 78rpm record of Horowitz playing Tchaikovsky, or Heifetz playing Prokofiev's second violin concerto on our prehistoric red vinyl 45's. To this day, I can't hear or play in the Prokofiev without twitching where the record needs to be turned over!

Playing the violin came easily enough to me, so all too often, I let other interests detract from the hours I probably should have been practicing. Anything electronic was infinitely fascinating to me, especially all those interior parts of radios. On some Saturdays, Dad drove me out to the original GI Joe's Army Surplus near Delta Park, where I reveled among the endless variety of obsolete electronic parts and gadgets. Huge vacuum-tube radio sets from ships, heavy old-style walkie-talkies, and bins full of resistors, capacitors, and diodes were a dream come true – a dream for what purpose I had no clue, but nothing could have interested me more. I ran a radio destruction zone in our basement, spending hours breaking things down or hooking parts up in some new configuration. Nothing I built ever worked as planned, but I enjoyed the pops and sparks when things went wrong.

By 13 and 14 years old, I was playing violin for many hours and many thousands of notes each week. Whether it was from my own practicing or rehearsing with the Junior Symphony, any normal day was another marathon of violin play-

Junior Symphony rehearsal at the Oriental Theater

ing. In my self-absorption, I thought everyone was somehow doing the same thing. What could be more important and more natural? After practicing my etudes though, another evening of sneaking a *Playboy* or blowing things up with my friend Greg next door seemed a normal course of mischief. I never thought much beyond that.

Entering Grant High School myself as a freshman in 1968, I always gravitated to the band room. Mr. Kaza usually had the orchestra in stitches with his humor and inspired with his natural passion for music. There was so much else going on at Grant too. Studying great things in algebra, geography and social studies also captured my curiosity, but everything seemed to be accompanied by all that music washing through me. Alongside my youthful crushes on girls in the band room, Sibelius just made those heartaches deeper and sweeter.

In freshman English, an unforgettable teacher, Mildred Eikeland, breathed life into Greek mythology almost as if she considered herself one more Greek Goddess. Staring into the far beyond, her eyes obscured by the glaze of her glasses, she rhapsodized the *Iliad* and *Odyssey* before us, her voice dramatic with emotion. I loved her teaching, and also that she took such an interest in my future with the violin. With her on my side, I lived (and practiced) to make her proud. Maybe the day would come that my Greek Goddess would be beaming at me from the audience as I triumphed through some concerto. It was easy to imagine.

In the Spring of 1970, the Junior Symphony went on its first European tour, visiting England, Italy and Portugal. Early impressions of London's Trafalgar Square, Florence's statues and bridges, and Lisbon's fish markets still remain in a hazy memory. One of our venues near London was the Camden School for Girls, which made quite the inspiring day for a 16-year-old boy. Socializing after that concert resulted in a pen-pal and an ensuing friendship that continues all these decades later.

Playing Brahms 2nd Symphony at the Camden
School for Girls

Returning to the United States through New York City, the Junior Symphony played a final concert in Alice Tully Hall at the Juilliard School. While there, I made sure to contact my Dad's sister, aunt Mort, who lived and worked on the upper east side of Manhattan. She was the head supervisor of surgical instrument and linens sterilization at New York Hospital. With one free evening to spend together, we took the train north to Bronxville, where my cousin Thomas Schmidt, another of Mort's nephews, was preparing for a piano recital.

A Yale graduate and phenomenal pianist, Tom played his entire recital for aunt Mort and me after dinner – a dress rehearsal of sorts. By the time my aunt and I returned to the Bronxville train station, the late night air had turned quite cold, and it seemed to me that aunt Mort had become especially quiet. To my shock, she suddenly fell to the platform suffering a *grand mal* epileptic seizure. Fellow passengers tried to console me, but I was shaking so much myself with the cold and surprise, I could hardly talk. After Tom and an ambulance came for aunt Mort, I returned alone to Manhattan with quite a story to tell my friends as we flew back to Portland.

Practicing in Alice Tully Hall at Juilliard. PJS 1970 tour.

From my sophomore year on, I attended the newly built John Adams High School in Portland. After more than a decade at Grant High, Mr. Kaza also transferred to Adams as its first instrumental music director. The school was experimental, and I did not do particularly well there academically with its less structured approach. We were encouraged to delve into studies of our own interests along with the school's emphasis on current events, racial issues and environmental concerns.

But I loved working on the school newspaper, the *Adams Unity*, and for one term served as editor. I was quite proud of an article I wrote on an Ethiopian exchange student. After my interview with the young man, the process to publication was fascinating.

Teenagers from Adams High School who were appreciated by Opitmist Clubs during Youth Appreciation week were: (L-R) Judith David-son, Marilyn Ness, Jane Fors, John Weller. Front: Donald Bilbrew, Rubie Wilson, Jim Sharpe, Nancy Vasquez.

Our paper always published a sports page, but any mention of music, dance and theater activities seemed to rate only an afterthought. As editor, I decided to right this wrong, and for one edition canceled the sports page that would normally have reported on the athletic heroes of the past several weeks. In its place, and with a certain lack of modesty, I created *Weller's Music Page*. Writing an editorial explaining the change, I designed a layout with stories extolling the month's activities in the orchestra, chorus and theater wing. I even reported on students taking ballet outside the school. After publication, an irate young man stormed the journalism room looking to take a swing at any editor who had dared desecrate the sports page. We talked him down somehow, and sports coverage resumed with the next edition.

I was a little small for my age and something of a late bloomer, but violin set me apart. My ability distinguished me from my schoolmates even as I envied their triumphs in sports and romance. Mr. Kaza's Hungarian blood got into me in those formative years. He demonstrated how violin could be played passionately and with abandon rather than as some military exercise or morose obligation.

My practice room during those years was our downstairs bathroom. I'd put the lid down on the toilet, the music on a stand, and there I'd sit through all my etudes. The adjacent wall still shows the myriad jab-marks from my bow. For all the thousands of hours sitting in the bathroom, violin was there to indulge in all that great musical emotion. And also of course, to show off! It was a power, and I could feel it in my hands.

At age sixteen, I won second place in the Oregon State Solo Competition playing the Bruch concerto. The following year in the spring of 1971, I took first place playing Wieniawski's *Polonaise Brillante*. This success earned me the concertmaster position in the

All-State Orchestra. It was the first time I ever sat as a concertmaster outside of my high school band room. During a rehearsal break at All-State, I discovered what the power of a violin can do.

While indulging myself in the passions of the Mendelssohn concerto, a stunning redhead from the orchestra, for whom I had developed a whopping crush, sat down to listen. With her chin resting on her hands, the wonder on her face told me I was playing directly to her heart. I could sing every word I wanted to say to her in that moment. It was so clear, so romantic and so easy.

Violin and I were already sky-high in rapture, but I was soon about to launch off the planet. With tremendously good fortune, I found myself transitioning for instruction to the brilliant violinist Elaine Richey. A Naumberg Competition winner, Mrs. Richey was a protégé of the great pedagogue Ivan Galamian, and had taught as his assistant at Philadelphia's Curtis Institute. She was currently on the

faculty of the North Carolina School of the Arts, but – as if by divine destiny – I had met her in the summer of 1969 at the charming Sun Valley Music Camp in Idaho.

Mrs. Richey showed me the moon. She channeled Galamian himself as she tweaked my vibrato and honed my bowing technique to perfection. By the summer of 1971, I was on fire with

Elaine Richey with violin students at Dollar Cabin, Sun Valley, 1971 her. I performed the Saint-Saens 3rd concerto at a student concert in the small Sun Valley Village Opera House, and Mrs. Richey was thrilled. She inspired me to five-hour practice days that were effortless and paid off with a vertical space-shot of technical accomplishment. I amazed even myself as I showered out a hybrid of Carl Flesch and Galamian three-octave scale systems in all their permutations, top of the fingerboard stuff.

I became a violin-playing machine that summer of 1971. My hands took on a warmth of symbiosis making them feel strangely indistinguishable from the violin and bow that they held. Vibrato went beyond technique and into its own world of color. Etudes by Gavinies and Dont, stylistic technical caprices, fell before me under Mrs. Richey's exquisite guidance. The caprices and etudes of Wieniawski, brilliant and violinistic, sizzled red hot under my piston rod fingers. Returning to Portland after Sun Valley, I was soaring high and just could not stop practicing. My senior-year high school photo ID shows a confident seventeen-year-old young man, ready to burst forth and conquer the world.

As violin and I were charging together into the future, high school began to feel like treading water. So what came next was the idea I might go off to college early and study violin big-time with a big-name teacher. The opportunity arose to study with the famous virtuoso Ruggiero Ricci, who was in residence at Indiana University at the time. Since I had once seen him perform with the Oregon Symphony, I almost presumed a special connection to him. And since Dad was Indiana-born, destiny seemed to be pointing me in that direction. IU had a school of music arguably on par with Juilliard and Curtis, so this was going to be a huge step forward. I felt primed and ready to make my mark as arrangements were made for a mid-December entrance audition in Bloomington. The plan that I'd leave high school half a year early was immensely exciting to me, as was the prospect that this would reflect well on my family and teachers in Portland. I recall a vivid and bizarre dream I had that fall, in which Ricci arrived on the front porch of our house in Portland. I dreamed a sense of pity for him, because I absolutely knew I could outplay him. Certainly that would not have been the case, but such was the degree of my subliminal confidence.

Rushing home from school by 1p.m. every afternoon that fall, I could not wait to put in another four to five hours of mega-watt practice before dinner. Each day was another stage of booster-rocket as I shot towards virtuosity. Invincible and self-assured, I powered and refined my way endlessly through my etudes, Wieniawski caprices, and the sonatas of Bach and Brahms. Most exciting of all, each day was a day closer to meeting Ruggiero Ricci, a day closer to the glory I knew I was about to forge with him.

During those last months of 1971, I also became engaged in Portland Civic Theater's production of *Fiddler on the Roof*, as The Fiddler!

This was already pure glory. Newspaper reviews noted how this production even had ". . . a real violin-playing fiddler on the roof." Thirty performances were programmed. Makeup professionals transformed my

John (L) with other Fiddler cast members

teenage face into the grizzled visage of the old mystical village fiddler. Taking that beard off my face every night got old. The spirit-gum glue they used hurt and gave me acne. But I didn't care. I loved every performance and I loved the life I was in.

The future was inevitable, violin my clear destiny now as it seemed I could conquer anything I practiced. I was on my way and loving every moment I could spend with the violin. I dreamed of tremendous adventures ahead, my eyes wide open as the most difficult and wonderful repertoire beckoned me forth. I practiced to the heavens, exulting in the sensations, the technique, and the sublime music itself. Intoxicated together in passion and completely obsessed with each other, violin and I had ascended into a rapturous and inseparable romance.

Unlike ever before, all this hyper-practicing resulted in a magnificent phenomenon developing on my left hand. A spectacular set of rock-hard calluses had taken bloom on my fingertips. They were bulbous and dense, protruding and distending above the fingernails. The surrounding flesh of the first joints rose up rigidly supporting what looked like large round knobs. Translucent to light and swelling from beneath, they throbbed curiously with life and just begged to be put to the violin.

After one marathon practice session, my pulsating calluses, grooved and shiny-black from the strings, looked so dramatic, so athletic, that I felt the need to show them off. Holding my hands up like a freshly scrubbed surgeon, I walked to the kitchen to show Mom what I had "grown". She shared my fascination with them. Giddy and proud of this transformation, I studied my calluses daily. They were part of the physiological mechanics that took my playing to these new heights, providing a solid and organic interface with the strings. I was acutely aware that my strength and accuracy on the violin depended on them.

During these weeks before the IU audition though, I began to notice how long it took to break in those calluses everyday. They needed to warm up to the strings to achieve that organic, virtuoso touch. My daily practice routine starting with an hour and a half of Carl Flesch scales and arpeggios always did the trick. My fingertips would soften from stone to something more leather-like, and I would then be ready to conquer more Wieniawski. But this routine gradually became annoying and time consuming.

I began to consider how to reduce the time frame by softening the calluses somehow before practicing. Filing them with an emery board was ineffective. I thought of soaking my fingertips in warm water, but worried the E-string might slice them through if I water-logged them too much. By the end of November the aggravation had reached an extreme.

I wanted to get to my caprices and concertos sooner than after almost two hours of mind-numbing scales and arpeggios. It seemed something had to give.

At seventeen years old, I was already grateful for a life that was good and rich with opportunities. Music, dance and excellent teachers had always surrounded my brother, sister and me. Mom and Dad had instilled in us a deep sensitivity to the arts and our place in humanity. I loved my family and friends, and now stood on the brink of some kind of greatness. I felt it was almost freakish how technically accomplished

I had become on the violin, how my singing and exalting through it seemed to know no bounds. My hands themselves looked physically beautiful to my eyes, especially with a violin in them. I was immortal and there was not a cloud on the horizon.

3

What I did next changed my life forever, derailing the trajectory of my dreams and veering me straight into a lifetime of regret. With all the unshakeable confidence of youth, I decided to trim my calluses down to some more comfortable level of thickness. I didn't consider what harm it could do since there seemed to be plenty to work with. But I did a clean job of it. Off they came entirely, with fingernail clippers, knife through butter. "That ought to do it", I remember thinking, "relief at last".

Taking another look though, my heart began skipping beats as I discovered what lay beneath: some sort of crinkly, pink and tissue-thin subcutaneous mush. The powerful shape and firmness I had developed collapsed to a flaccid pulp, and with nothing to support, the surrounding flesh atrophied almost instantly to Jell-O.

It didn't take but a moment with the violin to realize what I had done, and there was nothing gradual about it. The strings hurt right away, and I could only slip and slide out of control. Suddenly, I couldn't hold down any notes, much less double-stops, nor could I cover fifths, shift accurately or extend out of position. Attempting vibrato with fingers that turned to soggy marshmallow became a useless wobble. Only minutes before, I had raced up and down the fingerboard with pinpoint accuracy. But now my fingers could only splat down inaccurately in a pathetic mush.

In only these few moments of time, the violin mutated from a symbiotic extension of my own body to a totally foreign object in my hand. In one cavalier act of my own doing, I plunged from the top of the world to utter, nauseous, desperation. To my horror, I could no longer play the violin.

I couldn't play Yankee Doodle.

It looked and felt as if firecrackers had gone off on all four fingers. I was in big trouble, that much I knew. But I tried to believe I was not ruined, as I had no legitimate injury such as a broken bone or sprained tendons. The development of structure and calluses while playing a stringed instrument had seemed only a curiosity until now, not a particularly serious consideration in violin technique. My mind flooded with questions. Would this bizarre damage heal soon, grow back some firmness, or at least regain a layer of regular skin? What happened to my fingerprints? Should I practice as before to help grow the calluses back? A day went by, and then another...

I panicked to the pit of my stomach. The audition at Indiana University was only weeks away, plus I had a number of shows yet to perform at *Fiddler*. With desperate hope, I tried to proceed as planned. But I could only slip and slide pitifully on the violin strings, and even more painfully now as pinpricks of blood began to ooze from the raw meat at the ends of my fingers.

I had prepared the first movement of Wieniawski's D-minor concerto for the audition at IU, and on some level I could still slog my way through it. But it felt like I was driving on four flat tires. Any former command of the concerto was gone.

Playing even the simple *Fiddler* tunes was excruciating. My effort to find the notes or control vibrato, much less to rhapsodize those melodies, was unbearable. Somehow, in holy hell, I slipped and slid through those last performances. My run as The Fiddler, thus mercifully, came to an end.

As I tried to regain technical control, the most distressing and inexplicable collateral damage began to occur almost simultaneously. My bowing technique, my almost flawless Galamian bow arm which had always felt heaven-sent, began to warp and crumble as if in sync with the dysfunction of my left hand. What intricate psycho-motor coordination was destroyed, perhaps a neurologist could explain, but within weeks, it felt as if I had never held a bow before.

My five-hour practice days dwindled to a few minutes at a time of dread and futility. Together with my failing bow arm, practicing only exacerbated the rawness of my fingertips. It was an effort just to keep my heart beating or even draw breath. I could only scream and cry in the silence of my heart as my ability to play the violin pitched into a nosedive.

It felt too late to cancel the audition. Lannie Hurst, who played the role of Golde in *Fiddler*, had generously helped arrange financial aid for tuition and even bought me a pair of boots to help survive the Indiana winter. With all the expenses and expectations involved, I twisted in a hellish quandary. Who would believe this callus story anyway? In desperate denial, I tried to pinch myself awake as the audition loomed nearer.

Suddenly it was time to go, and I was scared to death.

4

December 1971

As the small commuter plane from Indianapolis descended toward the Bloomington tarmac, even stronger waves of dread surged through my petrified spirit. It was well below freezing in Indiana with crusty ice and pockets of snow covering the entire IU campus. Wearing my new boots, I found my way to the Indiana Memorial Union where I was to stay the night before the audition. I tried to practice, but my heart only sank deeper. No matter what I played, each note was a torture to control. The plush wood-paneled interior of the building dripped heavily with history and academia but its beauty only intimidated me as I made-believe tomorrow's audition could possibly turn out well.

The next morning, I crunched through the ice as I walked to the IU School of Music building. It was time to be judged. There they were in that small room – Ruggiero Ricci, Joseph Gingold, and other faculty members of the school of music. I recognized Ricci's short stature and unique face right away, from the concert in Portland and also from record jacket portraits. Joseph Gingold had been the beloved concertmaster of the Cleveland orchestra under George Szell before heading the violin department at IU.

The audition studio was acoustically dead with pegboard-style wall paneling, and it gave me no room for error. I wish I could erase from memory my cold, sweaty embarrassment as I fumbled and flailed my way through the Wieniawski. It was any musician's worst nightmare. Why had I done this to myself, why was I even here in front of these important people, what was I possibly thinking not to cancel the whole thing? I couldn't leave the room fast enough, slumping to the floor numb and catatonic in the hallway.

I thought that by any standards my audition had been a disaster. The audition committee was probably moved by my Herculean effort, but I was completely mystified that they actually accepted me. With hope so desperate though, I took their acceptance to mean that I should enroll at IU as a violin major and try to recover and excel under Ricci. It was probably the wrong thing to do. My instinct was of foreboding gloom, and I should have trusted it.

Returning to Portland, I tried glumly to celebrate Christmas with my family, and then began packing for my questionable move to Indiana.

January 1972

It was with a sullen and pessimistic heart that I returned to Bloomington, enrolled now as a violin major. I found my room in the Wright Quad dormitory and took the bed nearest the door. My roommate was a political science major from Syracuse, New York and a nice enough guy. It was mid-year at IU, so everyone else on the floor was settled in. There was laughter, blaring rock music and great spirit among my dorm-mates. Everything was perfect. Except for the detail that I could barely play the violin.

The campus was still covered by an icy glaze as I explored the grounds on the way to the music building. I was already shivering, but the sight of the unique cylindrical structure shook me even more deeply as I relived my audition there several weeks before. As I wandered the curved hallways, I could hear students already practicing and taking lessons. A stunning and polished Brahms concerto emanated from one studio, punching a terrific blow to my gut. I hadn't even taken my violin out yet and I already knew, I didn't stand a chance here.

I tried to practice, but it was no use. My sound-dead practice room with its unpleasant fluorescent lighting seemed only to emphasize my pale and emasculated fingers. It wasn't a matter of struggling with difficult music. Playing even a single note was a world of futility, with very little control over placement or vibrato. What could I possibly gain in this condition with instruction from anyone? Yet, here I was about to walk into a violin lesson with Ruggiero Ricci.

From the first moment on, lessons were an agonizing and embarrassing charade of going through the motions. For all the good it did, I soaked in Ricci's playing up close. But I can only imagine what he thought of me. I was in the room with him and doing my best posing as a violin major, but I wasn't really there; I was anywhere but there. I once lamented the issue with my calluses, but that seemed to go in one ear and out the other. Besides, what could he possibly do about it?

Ricci and I trudged through the Bach B-minor *Partita*, some movements of which can be played simultaneously as duets. But my fingers could only splat inaccurately on the strings while my psychotic bow arm attempted to falter along. I went blank. From deep within my stupor, Ricci's voice sounded barely audible, as if through a mile-long echo chamber. We plodded along through tiny-tot level trivialities as my heart ached for what I had been capable of not two months earlier. This was supposed to be glorious. Poor virtuoso Ruggiero Ricci, putting in his time with one more no-talent hack.

During one lesson, world-famous cellist Janos Starker from down the hall popped in complaining about his thermostat. Ricci and Starker fussed with the thermostat on the wall in our room, discussing its operation. There we were, the three of us, and these two mega-giants were talking thermostats. I was star-struck, but could only stand by mortified, miserable and irrelevant. The thought occurred to me, am I being punished for that cocky dream I had of Ricci back in Portland?

Not far from my dorm was a complex of humble white buildings called *Trees*. They may have been old army barracks but now housed many small practice rooms. Most of the rooms had what appeared to be brand-new Steinway and Yamaha grand pianos. I went to *Trees* often while at IU, preferring the isolation it provided from the intimidating music building. The futility of trying to prepare for lessons though went beyond exasperation. Pure dread now seized me each time I opened my violin case. I found that placing a tatter of old handkerchief under my fingers as I played helped ease the rawness of my fingertips. The material simulated, at least, something between me and the strings as the calluses had, and that's how I practiced every day. The rags always shifted around though and shredded into holes, so I collected a messy pile of remnants to draw from. I can still see my image in the practice mirrors at *Trees*: a left hand tangled in dirty white cloth, and a face in utter despair.

I had been assigned to the IU Philharmonic Orchestra, which performed at the opening ceremonies of the newly-built Indiana University Musical Arts Center. There were speeches and tributes, as well as an honorary plaque handed to the famous composer and bandleader Hoagy Carmichael who had written *Stardust* just off the IU campus years before. This first term at IU also had me trying to play in my first opera. It was Mozart's *Magic Flute*, and the depth of those beautiful arias tortured my aching soul, as actually trying to play the notes was so impossible.

On several occasions in the IU Phil, I sat next to an impertinent goof-off in the first violins. An exasperated Nicolas Harsanyi on the podium writhed in frustration as this fellow entertained us with pornographic things you can do with a violin. The troublemaker had rock-star good looks and a persona to match, but his attendance at orchestra rehearsals was sporadic at best. In my despondency, I consoled myself thinking "Well, this guy's going nowhere!"

IU had several other student orchestras on campus, and at some point I attended one of their concerts featuring the gorgeous Chausson *Poème* for violin and orchestra. To my utter amazement, that loser from the IU Phil strutted onto the stage and proceeded to play *Poème* like an angel. For an encore, he performed Paganini's 17th caprice with dash and perfection. I wondered how such a bad boy could play like that. It was Eugene Fodor. His stunning technique and flair was everything that I admired, and from then on I made a point to hear him whenever he performed at IU. Enthusiastically, I cheered him on. But on another level, my feelings were miserably conflicted. His immense talent and space-shot to stardom only put my own collapse into staggering perspective.

With everything to lose, I still tried to play the role of ambitious violin major. I attended Gingold's master classes where with envy I watched his talented students play the Sibelius concerto or a Beethoven sonata. And I tried to blend in when Ricci invited his students to spend an afternoon at his house for lunch and a dip in the pool out back. Ricci played through the Strauss sonata for us as it was upcoming on one of his own concerts, and afterward, I marveled at his priceless and stunning Guarneri as he placed it upon the piano. I knew it was one of the violins featured on his album *The Glory of Cremona*, which I had listened to endlessly in Portland.

It was something of a relief that on the many occasions Ricci traveled away to concertize, an assistant would fill in for him. With the extreme pressure gone, I could already begin to give up. My fingers as raw as ever, I was falling further into an abyss from which there seemed no escape.

The daily routine at IU provided no relief. As others around me went about their most exciting time of growth and discovery, I woke daily to a sense of hopelessness and bitter futility. *What in the world am I doing here?* I asked a hundred times to the small mirror inside my closet door.

As the months passed, I welcomed any distraction from the violin. Dorm life was a colorful and eye-opening wonder for my innocent sensibilities. The Rolling Stones' *Sympathy for the Devil* often blasted from across the hallway setting the mood for our weekly dorm parties that reeked invitingly of pot and beer.

As a music major, I took the standard requisites of music history and theory classes, and all majors were also required to pass a piano proficiency exam. With all those piano lessons behind me, passing

Clowning around in Wright Quad

the exam was easy, and piano became a place of comfort to turn when I couldn't stand the violin another moment. If I got a room with a piano at *Trees*, it was easy to spend at least half of my time there tinkling around with Rachmaninoff. It didn't seem fair; you don't need calluses to play the piano. My piano instructor, Marie Zorn, was impressed that I could manage a respectable C-sharp minor Prelude, most of which I could get through by rote memory.

The piano provided some degree of musical purpose with which to justify my enrollment at IU, but music history and theory classes depressed me. To my anguished thinking, they had nothing to do with actually playing music. I could work up no interest in these studies and did poorly in them. They seemed far afield from why I had come to IU at all, yet violin itself was already in full disintegration as a justification. Each day was empty of purpose and drive, a mockery of my dearest hopes and expectations.

As an elective, I had chosen Astronomy 101. I especially enjoyed this class, but perhaps mostly for its irrelevance to the violin. It had also been a boyhood hobby. I recalled freezing nights outside in our yard staring at the moon and the Pleiades through our small Tasco telescope. At IU, I got my turn at the large refracting telescope in the campus observatory and thrilled at seeing Saturn hanging in the night sky.

The white-bearded professor Edmondson delivered his lectures on astronomy by closed-circuit television to several thousand students watching from lecture halls in Bloomington and from other IU campuses scattered around the state. As the television monitors warmed up before each lecture, a selection of classical music always played intensively through the speakers.

Dr. Edmondson would then ring a bell for attention and begin: "For those of you who may be interested, that was *La Mer* by Debussy!" He would then speak rapturously about our ordered universe. Over time, I became so fascinated with his love of astronomy and music that I tracked down the studio on campus to watch his presentation in person. I felt that for his lectures alone it was worth coming to IU, so it was a pleasure to be able to tell him exactly that.

The ubiquitous bicycle subculture at IU was centered around the annual "Little 500" collegiate bike race. Eagerly drawn to the idea of biking everywhere, I bought a beautiful Gitane 10-speed, attended hands-on maintenance seminars and participated in several group outings into the countryside around Bloomington. The Gitane fit me like a glove. I biked solo all over IU as well, exploring the layout of the campus and areas beyond. I thought that if I just looked away from the violin for a time and taunted it with a little space while I biked in various directions, my technique might magically snap back to normal.

The Transcendental Meditation movement won me over, too. I thought that meditating might calm my grieving spirits. I received my mantra in a small ceremony, set aside time twice a day to meditate, and attended support meetings.

The meditating may have been calming, but my ability to play the violin only continued its plummeting death-spiral. Eventually I became very reluctant to mention my callus situation to anyone because it had been met with only blank stares and hunched shoulders. This was my own ordeal, and I could do nothing more now than to internalize it as my own dark and secret heartache.

5

I emerged panting and battered from my first semester at IU, and the summer break of 1972 arrived as a great relief from the pressures of having to play the violin. Josef Gingold had written a letter of invitation to attend the venerable Meadowmount School in upstate New York for the summer, but with sickening despair, I tossed it in the wastebasket. I began thinking I needed to get back to Elaine Richey, but what could I hope for even from her? That summer, the organizers of my old Sun Valley Music Camp had moved the entire operation to Banner Elk, North Carolina and renamed it the Sugar Mountain Music Camp.

Mrs. Richey lived in Davidson, North Carolina with her husband, David, and their three musically talented sons. David taught music composition at Davidson College, while Mrs. Richey taught violin at the North Carolina School of the Arts and also sat as concertmaster of the Charlotte Symphony. Mrs. Richey planned to teach at Sugar Mountain for the summer, so I made arrangements to escape from IU and beg her for salvation.

Arriving by Greyhound in the charming town of Davidson, I made my way to a small house Mrs. Richey had arranged for me to stay temporarily. The idea was to get a head-start on lessons before camp started, but I hardly played violin for her at all. Mrs. Richey was to play the Sibelius concerto with the orchestra that summer, so most of the time I spent with her was just watching her practice. I took solace in her playing, and she even seemed to value my point of view as she considered various phrasings and bowings.

Mrs. Richey was also open to my suggestions on driving a car. She had already failed twice to pass her motor vehicle driver's exam, so together we practiced maneuvers on the quiet streets of her neighborhood. It was refreshing to see the merely mortal side of Mrs. Richey. As I held on white- knuckled in her VW van, she tried earnestly to grasp the relationship between the clutch and gas pedals. Her face was set with determination as she practiced shifting gears in preparation for her next exam, but judging by our afternoon together, I have to assume she lurched to failure even the third time around.

Mrs. Richey was distressed over the death in the preceding January of her friend Michael Rabin. I saw Rabin play a recital in Portland just the previous year and gratefully received his autograph. The great violinist had died of a fall in his New York apartment attributed to a neurological condition. Mrs. Richey was upset though over rumors flying about of a drug overdose due to depression. She knew that he had been suffering, and this broke her heart.

Whatever the activity or conversation with Mrs. Richey that summer, I became quite adept at getting through the day without actually playing the violin for her. As Sugar Mountain Music Camp got underway, my overriding preoccupation turned to the romantic aspects of summer camp. Violin was a distant and distasteful excuse for being there at all. The weeks at Sugar Mountain were an emotional roller coaster both romantically and musically, so I just tried to survive the summer a day at a time.

As partial payment for my tuition at Sugar Mountain, I drove the camp's school bus, transporting students between the central campsite and their housing or to the concert venue in Banner Elk. It was straight forward, and I enjoyed the easy job. After one concert, I was trying to exit a crowded parking lot in the dark of night with a

full load of joyful students. After negotiating the entire length of the bus between rows of cars with only inches to spare, a rousing cheer went up as the bus drove into the clear. I felt quite the hero. But the very next morning, I got a sobering scare. I needed to turn the bus around in a three-point maneuver that included backing over a small bridge. I asked everyone to exit the bus for safety and to help guide me. As I headed up a steep slope to begin the turn, I realized too late that the air-brakes had not reached full pressure. As the bus careened backward, I could only approximate the location of the bridge. I missed, and the bus hit hard on the bridge railing putting a sizable dent in the rear bumper. I was lucky the railing held. It would have been about a fifteen foot drop backward to the river below.

I don't remember saying goodbye to Mrs. Richey that summer. There had been no fire and no excitement between us with the violin. Since I had successfully avoided lessons and practicing almost entirely, I had made myself irrelevant to her and had to accept that this was probably it between us. The summer faded uneventfully to an end as I slumped back onto a Greyhound and returned to IU.

On the home-front, storm clouds had been gathering well before I left Portland for IU, so it wasn't a total shock that Mom and Dad separated after many years of marriage. Dad had severed his ties with Concordia and St. Michael's, throwing our family into financial turmoil. He had found the hierarchy of the church leaning conservative and shallow in its theology, a fashion religion of piety and ironed robes. More frustrations also weighed on the marriage, with roots dating to our earliest days in Portland. Mom's physical beauty had always drawn leering eyes, ranging from Concordia faculty to colleagues doing community outreach with her. At some point she sought comfort in probably the wrong places.

After leaving Concordia, Dad found work teaching music at the Tongue Point Job Corps near Astoria, Oregon and commuted home on some weekends. After more than a year there, he quit when the prospect of a Job Corps center opening in Portland was assured, but the Portland location never opened. Scrambling for any income he could find, he began washing dishes at the Denny's restaurant a few blocks west of Lloyd Center.

About a year earlier, Dad had filled in for an ailing organist at Zion Lutheran Church in downtown Portland. During the eight weeks of the organist's hospitalization, Dad made quite an impression on the members of the choir and congregation of the church, and they remembered him when the original organist eventually retired.

While in his sixth week of washing dishes at Denny's, Dad was offered the position of organist and choir director at Zion, a position he held until his own retirement in 1992. Dad also found lifelong companionship with Trudy, a soprano in his choir at Zion, balancing and stabilizing his life for many years to come.

All along, Mom had been attending Portland State College in pursuit of a teaching certificate. At about the same time that Dad took over at Zion, Mom began a career teaching ethnic dance and vocal music in the Portland Public Schools.

Paul had entered Reed College in 1970 with academic honors, but under much pressure from the Selective Service, set school and cello aside to enlist in the army. He had been exploring his options as a conscientious objector, but by enlisting was able to opt for training as a medic. After basic training at Fort Lewis in Washington state,

Mom, Paul and Carol, 1972. Paul's eyes already look distant

Paul was stationed at various bases around the country for his medical training. He wasn't in the army very long though before symptoms of clinical schizophrenia began to strike him down. After only several years of enlistment, he was discharged and sent home to Portland.

As the voices in his head became louder and more frightening, he would sit on the dining room floor and stare at himself in our ballet mirror for hours on end.

My sister Carol was the one family member whose life seemed to be flourishing. She had never lost her passion for ballet and began a six-year tenure dancing with the Portland Ballet Company.

On most other levels, the innocent and hopeful years for our family were over forever.

6

Fall 1972

On my return to Indiana University after music camp, I was shocked and humiliated to find that Ruggiero Ricci had dropped me from his class. I was also profoundly relieved. Lessons with Ricci had become the last place on earth I wanted to be, and he had to know it. I had also been demoted to the "concert orchestra", a less prestigious group within the music school. My own assessment of my entrance audition the previous December was proving true. An emotional numbness was setting in as my ability to play violin could plunge no further. I was assigned to study with Harry Farbman, the catch-all violin teacher at IU and now I wondered why I remained in Indiana at all. Violin lessons were just an unpleasant and futile obligation at this point.

I was surprised to find that Eugene Fodor had been studying with Farbman while at IU and I wasn't sure what to make of it. Fodor had already studied with Jascha Heifetz, so I didn't understand the transition to Farbman. He probably didn't need to be taking violin lessons from anyone. As I arrived in Farbman's studio for another useless lesson one day, he was beaming with pride: "Gene just won the Paganini competition".

My mushy raw fingers, psycho bow arm and heavy depression had become my normal state of affairs, but my interest in violin was still gasping a last few breaths. I continued to attend Josef Gingold's master classes and various recitals on campus. Jacques Israelievitch played the most polished Handel sonata possible and Yuval Yaron's Paganini and Bach were flawless. Gingold himself played a luscious Wieniawski concerto on his Stradivarius. I sat only feet away, but in a world apart. I didn't belong here anymore.

In a small house right off campus I attended a rousing party thrown for Gingold's 63rd birthday. He was in his usual jovial mood. But I felt out of place, my own spirits glum and fearful. As I began slinking to a back corner of the living room, I was surprised to see Gingold heading straight for me. "Don't be such a wallflower!" he bellowed in his raspy and breathy baritone. My heart surged with his kindness, and I did my best to enjoy the rest of the evening.

The Vietnam War was raging in this era, with anti-war rallies and demonstrations in full swing across the country. With disintegrating hopes for violin, I sought comfort and escape in antiwar activities. My music theory teaching assistant was deeply committed to the campus protest efforts and found in me an enthusiastic recruit. I felt flattered and elevated by this lovely woman as she invited me to various rallies around IU. Soon, I was educating myself about the war's issues and offering to help any way I could. As I sat disheartened through Gingold's master-classes, my mind was mostly preoccupied with the next day's plans to distribute anti-war fliers and rally invitations.

The doors were bursting at one indoor rally with several hundred spirited anti-war demonstrators. A supporter had donated five bus fares to the upcoming enormous march on Washington, D.C., so we were invited to toss our names into a box for a drawing. As a relative newcomer to the effort, I felt both thrilled and embarrassed to hear my name called.

I soon found myself on the Washington Mall, chanting aloud with the IU contingent and marching along with my "Out Now!" placard. That demonstration in January 1973 was one of the last major protests of the war. On returning to IU, there was much interest from my dorm-mates in what I had seen in Washington. I realized I had participated in something worthy and historic, but the darkness of the Vietnam war colored the rest of my life and drew my interest forever to that part of the world.

Even this short separation from violin had been comforting. The futility of trying to restore my technique had beaten from me every last ounce of hope. I knew exactly what I had lost, and no amount of yearning was going to change that. The grandeur of the IU School of Music loomed as nothing but intimidation to me, and it was an unbearable agony that I could not rise to it.

For almost half of my life I had known violin technique on the most intimate and victorious terms. It had been so intertwined within my fiber that I took it for granted and assumed its ecstasy would always be there for me. The minute I cut off my calluses in Portland, I knew instantly and precisely the damage I had done. I remember closing my eyes and swearing an oath to myself in that very moment that I would get violin back, even if it took the rest of my life.

But that oath lay dashed in ruin. Even before my third and last semester at IU, I had seen the writing on the wall. My playing had only plummeted further into a perversion of itself, and in fact, my effort from the beginning at Indiana had been nothing but catastrophic.

It had been unthinkable that violin and I could die to each other. But now I could only fear, distrust and resent the violin. I had already begun to detest it. It had been long enough now to know, violin was not coming back.

Making the decision was a sickening relief. Surrendering a crushed spirit to fate, I packed my belongings, returned home to Portland, and quit the violin altogether.

7

Spring 1973

Without ceremony I buried my violin deep in Mom's basement. Out of sight and hopefully out of mind. Trying not to look back on my fall from grace, it was all I could do to try to forgive myself and move on.

Shaken and bitter with resignation, I cast about aimlessly for anything that might distract or allow me to move forward. Things were different all of a sudden and I had utterly no idea what to do next. Dark days turned to weeks and then to months as I helped Mom around the house, sat comatose through the Watergate hearings or just fiddled with my bicycle. In a daze, I biked near and far from Mom's house and wondered where life could possibly turn. As one useless day followed another, excruciating emptiness eroded all that was left of my spirit; even my life's essence felt as if it were shutting down with each passing moment.

By late fall, I figured that getting a job, any job at all, might offer some first step forward into the future. The Dairy Queen on Broadway, where Dad used to take Paul and me for Dilly Bars, wasn't hiring. But Meier & Frank, the large department store in Lloyd Center, took me on as salesman in the toy department.

Here I found purpose again, at $2 an hour. Redirecting my emotions, I dived headlong into this new world and familiarized myself with the many varieties of toys: Madame Alexander dolls, the Barbie line, Playskool, Tonka, Hasbro, all the various boardgames, plus an entire wall of small novelty toys. I became at one with the toy department and almost possessive of my turf. For the Christmas season, I set up the electric train display and kept the shelves stocked from the back room. I enjoyed helping customers with gift ideas, counted the day's cash after closing and recorded the checks.

The toy department had old-style manual cash registers but in time I was trained to work the new electric machines too. This skill elevated me to "Red Card" status, which meant I could provide break-relief for any other salespeople or be assigned to work in any other department. Besides toys, I began to work regularly in young men's fashions (Murphy & Finnegan), sporting goods, stationery, bedding, luggage, kitchenware, and even lingerie. To this day, I can fold a shirt in seconds to look as it did straight out of the package. One day, I was called out of stationery to help wrestle down a shoplifter, and on another occasion in Murphy & Finnegan, caught two men using a stolen credit card. The store manager himself came down to pay his compliments. But my spirit was still numb and I was deaf to his words.

This life was comforting. As time passed it distracted me from my fading thoughts of violin. I could feel in my gut the emotional process of letting go, but mercifully there were no more reminders of the past. Except for one, a final torture. Violin came back to haunt me one more time, and right there at Meier & Frank. It was a slow evening shift as I manned the register in luggage, and who should saunter past asking about handbags but Mildred Eikeland, my freshman English teacher. My Greek Goddess. She who had expressed such encouragement and hope. Unfortunately, she recognized me and I hung my head in shame as I told her my story. I wondered what she thought of my violin career now. Even as she wished me well, the humiliation was a final and defeating blow.

Before leaving Indiana University, I had made arrangements to ship my bicycle back to Portland. With any hopes for violin dead and gone, my original idea was to peddle it home all 2000 miles, come what may. But Dad thought the better of that and forbade me to do it. At least I had my beloved Gitane in Portland now, and I pampered it in the basement where I constructed a maintenance rack near an adjoining shelf for tools and oil.

It took almost half an hour to ride my bike to Meier & Frank from Mom's house. I cherished the memory that it was this very bicycle that I had bought in Bloomington and rode all over the IU campus. One evening after closing the register in toys, I returned to the bike rack to find it stolen. The loss put a hole right through me. It had been a good companion through difficult times. From then on I rode the bus to work.

Day after useless day I worked at Meier & Frank, wondering and wandering each day through. Somewhere along the line, I decided to enroll at Portland State University with the vague hope of settling into some new endeavor. My adviser recommended a general-studies major. This opened another world to me as I learned something about a variety of subjects. My trigonometry instructor was the perfect absent-minded professor with the shock of hair and thick-lensed glasses, but he made logarithms a thing of beauty. In American literature, my professor brought allegory to life, the message behind the story, and in philosophy, my brilliant professor took sober delight in cutting anyone off at the knees for not arguing a problem through with rational integrity. Along with geology and sociology, these studies outside of music, which I probably would not have taken at IU, made an important impact on me and greatly expanded what had been my terribly uninformed and narrow perspectives on reality.

While obtaining a SCUBA certification at PSU, I joined a swim class to improve my water skills. There I befriended a fellow student, Tony, from "South Philly". He was a square-jawed Italian Stallion and cool lady's man. Tough-guy Tony was a lousy swimmer, but he could chat up any woman anywhere. Tony lived in an apartment house he managed in southeast Portland. On account of our friendship, and since I could not afford a regular room, he offered the unfinished basement to me for $15 a month.

It was a chance to be on my own, humble a dwelling as it was. I furnished the place with shag carpet remnants and a black-light, just the style in those days. It was my first bachelor pad, so I didn't mind sharing it with silverfish and other crawly things.

Mostly I ate canned food heated on an electric plate borrowed from Mom, but I also splurged on meals at a nearby bowling alley, at the PSU cafeteria and at Sam's Hofbrau near the campus. My basement apartment was convenient to Lloyd Center, a reasonable commute to PSU, and a short walk to the bowling alley where I became a familiar face. Tony was mostly broke too, but it was cheap to cook up some spaghetti together, throw in a can of tomato sauce and call it dinner. Tony and I cruised southeast Portland often in his junker Impala, eying the streets for who knows what. We also headed to Lloyd Center where he would demonstrate his seductive skills on unsuspecting women. The arching bridge over the skating rink was one of his operating haunts, and his successes mystified and intrigued me.

I consulted Tony not only about the ladies but about spine and street-smarts. I have no idea what became of him, but his fearlessness was part of the fiber that rubbed off and came through for me later in life. And the basement apartment he made affordable for me became my headquarters as I explored other directions life had to offer.

I was hoping to date a young lady from my trigonometry class and was flattered that she walked the PSU Park Blocks with me. But I had little to offer her. It was depressing that all I did have was my employee discount on a stereo she wanted from Meier & Frank.

Perhaps that was her interest in me all along, which seemed to make the world that much more bleak a place. I could not seem to get beyond a pattern of lonely frustration and floundering.

A few months into 1974, my mode of transportation and new obsession turned to motorcycling. I bought a Honda 175 which seemed to fit my physical stature, and for hours on end I would hang out at Mark McCracken's Motorcycles near Lloyd Center. During particularly glum bouts of depression though, I took off astride the Honda on freeways to nowhere. I probably should have died several times over as just the speeds involved racing away toward Pendleton or Los Angeles felt therapeutic. Around a bend of deserted country road in Eastern Oregon, a large horned bull that seemed to come straight out of the ring in Barcelona stood dead center blocking my way. It was getting dark, and with about fifty miles of nothing  behind me I pondered my next move. It took a lot of horn-blowing and false starts to fake my way past him.

On the forested slopes of southern Oregon, I sped side by side with semi-trucks that drenched me on black rainy nights. Later, eaten alive by mosquitoes inside my modest tube-tent, I had to flee a pitch-black campsite around 2:30 in the morning. I bungled my departure though as the hastily loaded luggage shifted and the bike went right over. Banging up the left blinker and handlebar was a low point, but it was all part of my adventure and escape.

Passing through the San Francisco Bay area, I revisited our old house in Berkeley and contemplated the passage of time and events since living there. From outside the house, I stared at the windows of our old living room. It was right there, in another lifetime, that I had first opened a violin case.

Heading down Shattuck Avenue towards the university, I drove into a crazed panorama of hippies and flower children. "Cool bike, man!" crooned one especially shaggy fellow as he danced to the music in his head. For the second time in my life, I felt at home in Berkeley. It was still as enchanting as I remembered and would have loved to stay.

By the time I'd passed San Luis Obispo, I knew I had accomplished my escape. The faster and farther I sped away, the more my burdens faded and the brighter the future seemed.

Near Torrance, based on a friendly biker's local knowledge, I found a clearing by railroad tracks to throw down my sleeping bag. I had to curl up real tight when a pack of dogs came sniffing, and roaring freight trains throughout the night made sleep nearly impossible. The smoggy Los Angeles freeways and dreamy California beach scenes lured me up and down the coast where I was seduced by the sights and climate of southern California. Observing a group of teenagers effortlessly body-surfing, I wondered how hard it could be. It took only one attempt to discover I had no idea what I was doing.

Crawling out of the pummeling surf on all fours and coughing out about a gallon of seawater, I collapsed, together with my dignity, to the sand.

When riding the motorcycle, I always wore a helmet. But returning up the Sacramento Valley that summer, it was much too hot to wear my protective leathers. Riding bare-chested was exhilarating, but I soon discovered what bugs feel like at 70mph.

Mom thought the motorcycle idea was suicidal, but I craved the carefree and often reckless adventure of it.

Not much more to lose.

8

Fall 1974

Back in Portland, classes resumed at PSU and I returned to work at Meier & Frank. I also made a move from the basement into a small studio upstairs in Tony's apartment house. The rent rose to $55 a month, but it was definitely a step up. Life achieved a level of normalcy. I had a job, I was back in school, and I had a real apartment. It also felt like the right time to stash the motorcycle in Mom's garage after I found a mostly-wrecked forest-green 1969 Toyota Corolla for $650. The four wheels under me felt safer than the motorcycle, so this made Mom a little more comfortable too. I adorned the shelf under the rear window with a swatch of shag carpet from the basement and fantasized that the car was some sort of love-mobile, even with its unpainted right fender and impotent performance.

Murphy & Finnegan, the men's fashions shop in which I worked so often at Meier & Frank, was situated directly across a walkway from the store's snack bar. During breaks, I occasionally enjoyed the flirtations of the attractive young lady there turning hot-dogs.

It felt so inevitable. Portland State was hosting a horror film festival that provided the perfect opportunity to ask her out. We watched what I still consider to be the most frightful horror film I have ever seen. My date and I left the theater grasping each other in such a terror, there was no separating us and no possible place to go other than back to my apartment.

Finally, a connection. It was tender, but a little desperate after that horror movie. We all remember our first time. I remember mine as an affair between a pants salesman and a snack bar girl.

My efforts in academics were sincere, yet they felt aimless. After about a year at Portland State, I asked my adviser if I might shift toward a degree of some kind in medicine. Since my brother Paul had been training as a medic in the Army, the field intrigued me. I found myself suddenly buried in the minutiae of chemistry and biology, much of it difficult to absorb as I had no previous schooling in those sciences.

Excited with my new goals in medicine, I volunteered as an orderly for the emergency ward at Portland's Providence Hospital. It was probably a naïve move, but the effort did get me straight into a hospital. I found myself thrilled with the moment to moment routine of the trauma center. There were the slow hours of tending to the elderly, but I got an eyeful of many nasty injuries as well. Most of these patients I wheeled down to X-ray or up to their room in the hospital. I was asked to make up the beds and help lift patients with a sheet from one to another. It was also my task to take sick elderly men to the bathroom with all that entails.

I loved the ambiance of the hospital and developed great respect for the science behind the medical profession. As lowly as I was, I felt privileged to be in that important place. Wearing my white smock with "John Weller, Volunteer" pinned on the front swelled my heart with purpose. It was an honor to be recognized as an orderly, even if only being asked for directions in the hallway.

An emergency call from an ambulance crackled over the radio that a severely injured woman was on the way. The poor lady had been hit by a car and came in bloody and unconscious. The orbital area around her left eye had been crushed and she was bleeding profusely from all over her head. The doctor leading the trauma team probed her eye socket with gloved fingers, and at least six more doctors and nurses attended to her many other injuries as well. Her clothes were scissored off in seconds and tubes were inserted everywhere while the portable X-ray machine was wheeled in. During this process I was asked to hold onto two pair of forceps that were squeezing off some of the bleeding at the top of her head. Over the course of about an hour, they got her stabilized and the professionals began leaving the room one by one.

For a very few amazing minutes, I found myself alone in the room with this woman. It was just me, with no medical training, leaning on my elbows at her head and holding dearly onto those clamps. When I was relieved, I looked at the blood on my hands. I considered it there a badge of honor and something stirred inside me. It had been a long time: I felt pride.

So this was it, I realized. This was life without the violin.

By the end of 1974, my glory days with violin had faded to over three years in the past and a million miles away. I dared not think back on them, as I felt nothing now but intense loathing for the violin. I couldn't even remember my years of ecstasy anymore. I knew I would never play again, much less even try. The very thought of violin and anything to do with classical music had turned repugnant, and even a chance recognition of Beethoven or Shostakovitch on the radio would send me into a nauseous shiver. The more I detested the violin for destroying my life, the better I could cope, the better I could forget.

A new circle of friends had evolved during these recent years, comprised of a few classmates from Portland State, some co-workers from Meier & Frank and Providence Hospital, plus a few locals at the bowling alley. They knew nothing of my past life with the violin. On the other hand, Eugene Kaza and Elaine Richey must have thought I'd dropped off the planet. That bothered me deeply, but I just could not look back and admit my fate to them. I hoped to high heaven never to cross paths with anyone who might ask what had become of me. The passage of time provided comfort, and I had long begun to heal and put to rest the trauma of quitting the violin.

A sad calm of acceptance and wonder descended upon me as I looked back at what had been a magical run with the violin. Life now offered other possibilities. With youth on my side, I had a shot at an academic education and everything else the future had to offer. There were no more self-centered hours of practicing toward some vague career of bowing strings over a wooden box. As the calendar turned to 1975, here finally was the silver lining.

I was free of that damn violin at last.

Photo Gallery

Photo Captions page 133

MEET THE PLAYERS 7

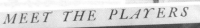

DAVID BRYANT, 19, is playing his first concert as principal flute. With this post also comes the privilege of using the fine Powell flute which belonged to former first-flutist Carol Fogdall. Her parents have loaned this instrument to the JS in her remembrance. David is a student at Clark College, in Vancouver, Wash. and studies his instrument with John May.

SANDRA CUSHMAN, 20, attends the University of Portland where she is majoring in music and studies the violin with Anthony Porto. As assistant principal of the second violins she shares one of the biggest responsibilities in the Orchestra — that of training the section with the most new players. This is her sixth season in the JS.

MARY ANN COGGINS, 21, is concertmaster for this program and the recent Christmas concert. Her appointment to share this responsibility was made in recognition of her marked progress in the past two seasons. Last summer she was the Orchestra's delegate to Tanglewood where she held the first chair in the Institute orchestra. She has played in the JS for six years and studies the violin with Raphael Spiro.

JOHN WELLER, 12, is the youngest member of the Orchestra and occupies the last chair of the second violins. For his entering audition, however, he played the Mozart Concerto #3, which many of the first violins played. Both he and his brother Paul entered the JS last fall. John attends Kennedy School and is a violin pupil of Eugene Kaza.

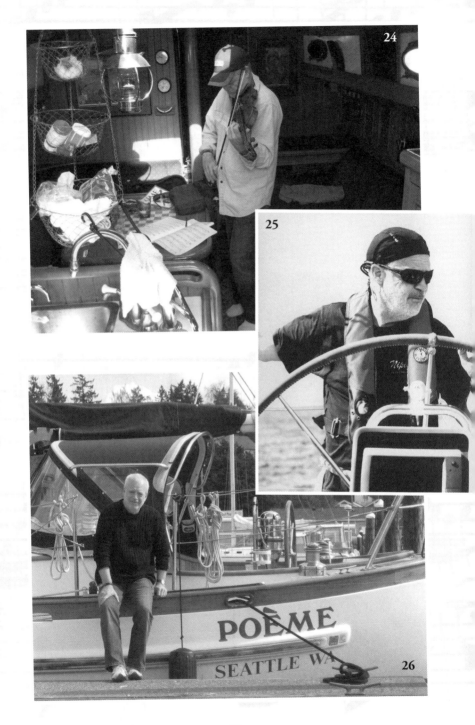

9

You need to get back to the violin! You were way too good to abandon it altogether!

The chance meeting outside the cafeteria at Portland State paralyzed me on the spot and I could only respond with a dumb stutter. Even in high school, I had hardly known this fellow Tom Raimondi. Now after only three minutes he was frantically lecturing me about returning to the violin. Just opening the old wound, and I could only roll my eyes. With life now heading in other hopeful directions and violin forever banished, I resented his presumptive intrusion.

Tom was dumbfounded that such a capricious injury could have destroyed my ability to play the violin. But what could he possibly know? I began to recall Tom as the straggler who hung around the band room at Adams High, trying at nearly a beginner's level to play the violin. I winced at my own vague memories of him as quite the klutz on the violin, and also as remarkably tone-deaf. I had no interest in pursuing the subject with anyone, but especially not with him. Losing a passion this primal and this technically demanding was beyond my ability to explain and beyond my emotional capacity to confront again at all. How could this naïve and oblivious fellow possibly understand what I had suffered? I resented Tom's obnoxious enthusiasm and silently cursed having crossed paths with him.

Tom, though, seemed to take our meeting as a design of fate. His conversation was engaging and left me no choice but to acknowledge his sincerity. What I did not recognize about him right away was his brilliant natural intelligence, a profound character and tremendous innate kindness. Tom's depth and sensitivity to life plumbed my own as we began to talk of the events of the past several years. He was clearly my intellectual superior, and it wasn't long before he had me feeling quite inadequate by comparison.

As fellow PSU students, Tom and I met occasionally and gradually forged an easy-going friendship. Through humor and laughter, we talked philosophically about life, and developed a mutual respect we hadn't known in high school. Even with an aversion for violin still this intense, I felt grateful as he spoke of his own love of music and of his admiration for my playing years before. It was becoming clear that Tom, who never played well himself, saw my early triumphs as his own on some level. His unpretentious nature made his words and ideas that much more powerful, and I began to listen with interest and wonder.

Over the next few weeks, Tom became relentless about my returning to the violin and would not let it go. For every optimistic idea he put forward, though, I had an overwhelming argument against it, so we usually ended up in stalemate. I was not about to put myself through another round of self-annihilation. Everything I had been as a violinist was destroyed, and I had just spent the last two years since Indiana running in the opposite direction.

Even in the face of my resistance, Tom drew what he thought was a credible scenario. He suggested that I make an effort to play the violin again, as slow and painful as that might be, with the goal of auditioning one day for the Oregon Symphony.

Tom had no idea what he was asking me to do. But these conversations stirred my deepest yearnings. *God* I wanted to play again, but the quandary it presented was a torture. The very thought of approaching violin at this stage stirred to life again a deeply-suppressed trauma. The agony and futility of IU still lay scorched in my memory, my last moments with the violin warped and nightmarish. The thoughtless act that had dashed my dreams to hell still made no sense and I saw no path forward for violin and me in this lifetime.

But gradually, I began to lose my arguments with Tom. Despite a rising dread and despite my determination never to face the violin again, I began to warm to his vision. Was it this good friend's faith in me, or his naïveté perhaps, that finally persuaded me to exhume my violin from Mom's basement.

The day came that I drove to Mom's house, walked through the kitchen, descended the stairs to the basement, and searched along the wall behind the furnace. Musty and silent, there it was.

Gazing into the case, it was all I could do to stifle the tormenting memories.

"Hello again violin, remember me?"

10

It was early in the spring of 1975, and my fingers had long since healed over and regained a layer of regular skin. While there was no firmness at all and no surrounding structure, at least I had my fingerprints back. Holding my breath, I took up the violin again, and cradling it guitar-style, studied at length the feel of the strings under my fingers.

What I discovered right away was that my fingers did not slip on the strings as before. The layer of skin held on, if tenuously, from one note to the next and with some sense of placement. With no developed structure, covering fifths was almost impossible, but it seemed at least I could try.

When the time came to set bow to string, my attempts to play were excruciating. But I was expecting that. Trying to control the slippery bow felt even worse and angular than I remembered. The damage, no less psychological, had been done. I had lost the touch and could only grapple for control with sprawling fingers. Both hands were feeble and disoriented, and with no technical strength, the violin and bow felt horrible trying to play even single notes. Old familiar pangs of panic began to set in, and I felt little hope of anything coming of this. But slowly, incrementally, molecularly, I tested what I could do.

The simplest exercise of playing one note to another took all my concentration, and my old Carl Flesch one-octave scales helped set a routine as I experimented with drawing a tone again with the bow. Any subtleties beyond simply back and forth eluded me, but I kept a picture in my mind of how I had practiced with such effectiveness back in 1971. Moving gradually and carefully into three-octave scales and slow arpeggios, I tried to color my tone with vibrato. Shifting up and down the fingerboard again felt like exploring old familiar territory. I felt that, at the least, I knew what I was trying to do.

Dusting off some old Bach and Kreutzer, a sense of mission developed. Day by day, then week by week, I decided to hold on tight.

While practicing in front of a mirror, I studied every motion and tried to reconstruct a hazy old lost technique.

Occasionally, Tom came over with his own violin while I stumbled along. He still wanted to play, and saw this as an opportunity to learn violin alongside me. I owed him at least this much, to guide him as best as I could in his desire to improve. It was frustrating though. As full as he was of life and laughter, Tom's face went strangely blank, his torso stiffening, the moment he placed the violin under his chin. The idea of searching for beauty of tone seemed to escape him, and my sanity tangled in upon itself at his question "how can you tell if you're playing in tune?"

As awkward as the violin and bow felt physically in my hands, I could see nothing particularly wrong with my form in the mirror, except my absurd bow-grip. There was no firmness to my fingertips, but the healthy layer of skin now gave me hope that practicing might actually amount to something.

It was a lonely crawl. There were no teachers or graduation recitals to prepare for, no performance certificates to earn. No one was listening. I was on my own. But as a vague sense of familiarity began to return, the sweetest aching imaginable began to emerge from my depths. Recalling my earliest musical impulses, the natural joy of playing the violin was tearing through my spirit all over again. Why did violin have to come crashing down the way it did; could I possibly love it again so simply as before? The floodgates burst open, and I knew exactly what I wanted to do and felt so compelled to do. Could it be that I was actually trying to sing on the violin again?

And was it Elaine Richey that I felt, smiling over my shoulder every step of the way.

Old instincts kicked in as I tried to refine my scales and etudes. To keep up the momentum, I ordered books of orchestral excerpts and studied specific recordings of music that might be useful for an audition. So much flooded back as the flow and passion for the violin began to surge through me again. I wondered if the violinist inside me had just been lying dormant as I wasted away in Murphy & Finnegan or held onto those bloody clamps in the emergency room.

Fall 1975

Despite my well-developed sense for doom, I gathered the courage to contact the Oregon Symphony and was granted an audition. Around the same time, I requested an audition with the Portland Opera as well.

One week to the day before the symphony audition, I played for Stefan Minde, the conductor of the opera. Stefan was very kind and encouraging but informed me there was no position available in the opera orchestra at that time.

It was true, no doubt, but I took this as the rejection I had anticipated and deserved. Moreover, if I couldn't qualify for the opera orchestra, which plays in a pit, I decided there was no chance of winning a symphony position one week later. Hopelessness was nothing new to me: That night, even as Tom tried to console me, I belted *Colt 45's* to the brink of unconsciousness.

I had all the next week to stew about the upcoming symphony audition, my March to the Gallows. The sense of inevitable failure was overwhelming, but perhaps that actually helped relieve the pressure.

The day of the audition arrived, and to this day I cannot believe the impossible outcome. For the first time since cutting off my calluses almost four extremely hopeless years before, the winds of fortune turned in my favor.

11

Tom and I screamed and turned cartwheels.

This was impossible. I had landed a position with the Oregon Symphony. Conductor Lawrence Smith put me in the back of the second violins, on the last stand, inside chair. It was the farthest back you can go, but I was ecstatic beyond words. In a whirl of delirium, I knew exactly what this meant: This was life after death.

Any plans other than of trying to recapture a future with the violin went out the window. I immediately polished up my violin and began shopping for a tailcoat and black shoes. An envelope arrived by mail from the Oregon Symphony containing the rehearsal and concert schedule for the season, plus detailed information ranging from health insurance to concert dress codes. It was an ordinary packet of information to start off the season, but I studied the contents as if they were scrolls revealing the secrets to immortality.

Arriving for my first rehearsal, it was with fear and trembling that I made my way to the upstairs rehearsal hall in Portland's Civic Auditorium. My heart wanted to celebrate as I sat down in an orchestra again after all this time – and a professional one at that – but my mind scrambled with confusion. From the back of the orchestra I had to wonder, what is this thing, who are these people, how can I possibly belong here? I knew that I was there by the skin of my teeth and out of my league. It seemed more likely that I should be doing another shift in kitchenware about now.

I was right where I wanted to be, but my hands ached in protest. My ability to play felt utterly frail and hanging by a thread. My bow grip remained tenuously out of control, and covering fifths was still a challenge with my undeveloped fingertips. I just held on the best I could as my fingers tried to gain strength and accuracy. Symphony rehearsals and concerts are invariably violin marathons, and I nearly crumpled under the pressure right away. With the structured schedule though, I kept building on that thread and, desperately happy, pushed forward.

After nearly two years at Meier & Frank, I was more than ready to leave, but I still owed the store about two more weeks of work. During this interim, a co-worker and I working sporting goods together were discussing an upcoming Oregon Symphony concert. Rick was a music aficionado and seemed to keep himself on top of the local scene. This particular program featured a soprano he admired, and he asked if this concert was one I would consider attending. I know that I stunned him speechless when I told him that not only was I going, I was playing in it. I felt guilty springing it on him this way, but it was so sweet to say the words. I soon left Meier & Frank forever.

Trying to recapture my former command and technical control was to prove painfully elusive. The daily challenge at the symphony became in fact a matter of holding on for dear life, a matter of simply not dropping the bow to the floor. Keeping up was agonizing as I mentally drew on everything I could remember from the past. There were horrible days when my hands would not work, but there were also days of triumph. Moments of control and passion would blossom and then be gone. But when it happened, I knew it, I felt it, I remembered it, and my heart would soar with hope.

In the back of the Oregon Symphony, 1975-76 season

As these first weeks and months passed, I began to reflect deeply on this new life in the symphony. There I sat in a major orchestra as if nothing had happened, as if this were some inevitable step forward as a musician. But the gaping wound in my heart was still gushing, and it was all I could do to keep my secret of the last four years concealed. Night sweats plagued me with doubts about my ability to play and whether I was entitled to this turn of events at all. On the surface it seemed the nightmare had been lifted from me. But I had seen oblivion. I had to think that what those years of sadness did to my face would be obvious to anyone.

It wasn't long though, before I ran head-on into one of life's great lessons. From the beginning of the season, we played back-to-back children's concerts by the dozen. Thousands of kids were bussed in from around the area in screaming masses. They were getting their first tastes of Beethoven's Fifth or Benjamin Britten's *Young Person's Guide to the Orchestra*. My heart would break as I noticed another group in the audience, positioned in their wheelchairs across the front row. Young patients with muscular dystrophy, cerebral palsy or other severely debilitating afflictions were wheeled in to hear the mercifully beautiful music. With twisted bodies and gnarled hands, some would writhe and bark "inappropriately" during the concert. Most tried to flop an enthusiastic applause as best they could. Who are these souls, I wondered, suffering an oblivion from which there is no escape? I looked at myself playing the violin and blistered inside, *how dare I ever pity myself again.*

My first season with the Oregon Symphony passed quickly. On the first day back the next fall, the personnel manager informed me that I had been promoted to the first violin section. I had to think it must have been my enthusiasm back there on last stand. It must have been apparent, my desperate gratitude to be in the picture at all. To be playing the violin again, at all.

During the next three seasons, I found myself more in the forefront, playing in the many varieties of concerts presented by the

Oregon Symphony: Classical, Pops, and Children's concerts were all performed at the Civic Auditorium. The Pops with Norman Leyden were among my favorites especially while playing his exquisite arrangements from his days with Glenn Miller: *Moonlight Serenade*, *Frenesi*, and *Mood Indigo*, among other big-band numbers. These melodies colored my mood as much as any Debussy or Bartok we played at classical concerts. Leyden originally came to Portland as guest conductor of the Portland Junior Symphony during Jacob Avshalomov's sabbatical leave. I had played for Leyden then – I was about fourteen years old – so playing for him again was like closing a circle. Bus tours around the state, tuxedos, the music, colleagues: this was symphony life, and I cherished it all.

Doors continued to open as I became active outside the orchestra. As reluctant lead violinist in the Harold Lawrence String Quartet, I played at Riddles Tavern downtown every Thursday evening. My hands were not really up to the first violin parts, but we had a respectable following. It was quite a casual affair as we played Mozart, Dvorak, and Haydn quartets, all while nursing pitchers of beer at our feet. Working in the symphony, the quartet, and odd jobs all over town, violin felt back in my life. Ready or not, I was playing again.

As thrilled as I was with this second chance at violin, I still grieved for having lost track of Elaine Richey. By 1976, I hadn't seen her in four years and could only think back on her with deep remorse. It was she, after all, who had sent me to the moon. I wanted fervently to make peace between us and once again entrust my playing to her. I discovered that she was teaching summers at Utah's Snowbird Music Festival, so I gathered my courage and drove to the mountains outside Salt Lake City.

I had not contacted the festival though or let her know I was coming. It was deeply embarrassing that I could not play up to my old standards, and arriving incognito gave me a way out. Wandering the Snowbird grounds, I ran head-on into the festival's orchestra conductor Christian Tiemeyer, who had taught cello during my summers at the old Sun Valley Music Camp. He remembered me and, ignoring my story of gloom, insisted I join the festival. The kindness of his invitation almost broke my heart.

Meeting Mrs. Richey again was bittersweet, but I surrendered myself to her again and tried to make her proud. I resumed private lessons and also joined with other fawning students who attended her informal master-classes. I learned all over again the depth of her love for the violin and its technique. Any time spent with her was more than healing. She taught a vision that I had lost track of, and I drank it in as the nectar of life.

Mrs. Richey's husband had come to Snowbird from North Carolina that summer for recreation. David was generous with his time and treated me to his thoughts on musical composition. As we strolled the grounds of Snowbird, he spoke eloquently about what he viewed as the true ingredients of music. He felt that he could taste music, and sniffing the air, could smell it and sense its color. These were the senses he used as his own compositions took form on the page. I seemed to be studying with two Richeys that summer, and I could not have asked for more.

On a student recital held in a Snowbird conference room, I had the opportunity to play a short piece for violin and piano, *Valse Bluette*. It was all I could handle, but for the first time since Sun Valley five years before, Mrs. Richey once again seemed thrilled. "It's hard to play a short piece so well" she said, "you only get one quick shot at it". The piece was barely two minutes long, but it was technically all over the violin and romantically stylistic. The short performance marked a milestone. A few minutes of making Mrs. Richey proud gave me inspiration for another year of hope and optimism.

When it came to Mrs. Richey, my pattern had been to chase her from one summer camp to the next over the years. In the next summer of 1977, I returned to Snowbird to study with her once again.

While I was still plagued by unrelenting awkwardness and bungling, Mrs. Richey worked her magic. As distrustful as I still felt of my abilities, I won the festival solo competition with the Chausson *Poème*. Mrs. Richey had played *Poème* the first summer I'd met her so long ago in Sun Valley, so this performance meant everything to me.

At my first rehearsal with the Snowbird orchestra, my hands went rubbery with stage fright and my knees shook and buckled. But I knew the piece well and was determined to play it beautifully for Mrs. Richey.

Rain was falling gently on the Snowbird concert tent with rumbles of thunder in the distance. What a mood it set for this music. Somehow the stars aligned as my hands and heart sang out the haunting beauty of *Poème* on the Festival's final concert. It was a pinnacle moment for me.

But Mrs. Richey missed the highlight of my life. Earlier that week, David had suffered a stroke back in North Carolina. She rushed to him of course, but he died shortly thereafter.

After that summer at Snowbird, violin and I made our way into the future alone.

I never saw Mrs. Richey again.

12

Summer 1978

Recalling the letter of invitation Josef Gingold had written for me at IU in 1972, I tried to fulfill my childhood dream of attending the Meadowmount School in upstate New York. This was a summer camp at which young violinists labor through mandatory five-hour practice days toward fame and fortune. It was still with a degree of trepidation that I enrolled and made my way to New York.

Gingold's old friend and colleague Ivan Galamian had created this place, and most every world-class violinist had passed through there at some point. At age 24 I was just about everyone's older brother, but I went through the motions as well as I could and lived vicariously through the young virtuosos who abounded there.

Meadowmount School of Music
R.F.D. NO. 2
Westport, N. Y. 12993
IDENTIFICATION CARD
JULY - AUG., 1978
John Weller
ADDRESS: Portland, Oregon 97211
SIGNATURE:
BIRTHDATE: 1/23/54

It was mostly out of curiosity that I attended Meadowmount. I wanted to experience this place that drew the best of the best. A few of the students tried to set records for the most hours practiced within a 24-hour day. Some of them wore bandages trying to keep their tendonitis under control.

One day, to my surprise, word came that Gingold himself had arrived at a motel in nearby Elizabethtown. He had come to Meadowmount to relax and teach a master class of his own. Perhaps I was the only one available at the moment, but of all people, it fell to me to drive the camp car to "E-town" and pick up Gingold at his motel. Awful memories of Indiana University raced through my head as I drove the highway toward town. With my history of failure and embarrassment at IU, I had hoped to leave the past behind, and certainly never have to explain myself to Gingold. Arriving at the motel and knocking on his door, I broke into a sweat. Five years had passed, but I worried that while escorting him to the car he might even vaguely recognize me. I acted the total stranger though, and we had the most delightful drive back to Meadowmount. Just to ensure my anonymity, I sat in the back of the room during his master class. I was glad that, even as strangers, my last personal moments with Gingold had been pleasant and lighthearted.

Ivan Galamian attended all the spectacular performances at Meadowmount that summer, and half the applause always seemed aimed in his direction. Galamian was in his final years, but there he was, proudly surveying his latest crop of geniuses.

And hanging on the cafeteria wall photo-gallery, there among some of the greatest names in recent violin history, was his protégé and the heroine of my life, Elaine Richey.

That same summer of 1978, the phone rang with an invitation out of the blue to join the Alaska Music Festival in Anchorage. I couldn't say yes fast enough.

It was the first of three short summer festivals I enjoyed there. I made good friends along the way, both with my home-stay family and with the musicians of the orchestra. Many of these musicians were up from the Seattle Symphony. In our spare time we were able to enjoy much of what Alaska had to offer. Drives and hikes into the countryside as far as the town of Homer and Portage glacier drew us together as a close musical family. After concerts, we would head into Anchorage, often ending up at the Monkey Bar, a place somewhat on the rough and tumble side. After one raucous evening, we emerged to find the car we had borrowed from our host family towed away. We hadn't noticed the "2 to 5 a.m. No Parking for Street Cleaning" sign. I can't quite recall how we got home that night, but we took care of retrieving our host's car from the city impound the next day.

My friends from Seattle soon began encouraging me to audition for the Seattle Symphony. It was an attractive idea, but I still felt that my acceptance by the Oregon Symphony had been a fluke. The prospect of another audition stirred the usual fears within me, but the seed had been planted. After the Alaska Festival ended, most of the Seattle people rushed home to begin their rehearsals for Wagner's *Ring* cycle. My return was more leisurely. I boarded the Marine Highway System ship *Columbia*, but not before making plans to visit my friends in Seattle while returning to Portland.

In Seattle, I found myself ambling around Seattle Center as I waited for my friends to finish their Wagner rehearsal in the Opera House. I was seeing Seattle for the first time and was easily drawn into contemplating the possibility of a life there. Sitting on the rim of the International Fountain and enjoying its smooth warmth under my hand, I squinted up at the Space Needle. My heart raced at the thought. If only, I dreamed, could I find myself in this picture.

An opportunity to audition came in the fall of 1979, and I put everything I had into it. Auditions were held then at Brechemin Auditorium in the University of Washington music building. As beautiful as the campus looked that day, I was a nervous wreck. I knew very well how all the orchestral excerpts went, but nerves got the better of me. With my relentlessly problematic bowing technique, the string-crossing passages in Mozart's 39th symphony threw me into a tailspin. Rather than following the contour of the arpeggios in unison, my arms went opposite each other like a squawking goose. I probably sounded about the same. But recovering from that embarrassment, I was fortunate the audition committee then sat through my effort of the entire Ysaÿe *Ballade*. Conductor Rainer Miedél put me into the first violins. Although there were painful ties to cut from Portland, I was once again giddy with disbelief as I entered the Seattle Symphony and Opera orchestra.

The Oregon Symphony schedule had been busy enough, but the Seattle Symphony schedule dwarfed it by far. Once again, I found myself barely hanging on for the ride. We were playing *Don Juan* and

La Mer right away, two of the most difficult technical challenges for violin. Fortunately, I had practiced them for my audition and could almost pull my own weight, but my heart wanted to play over the top. My fantasy was to play as I used to, but my hands lagged behind. I had no option but to persevere. Early in 1980, auditions were held for positions on the second stand, and Miedél granted me the lofty third-chair position, Assistant Concertmaster. I was 26 years old.

In April, the symphony tour to Europe had me suddenly front and center in Vienna, Munich and Lugano. My hotel-mate on that tour was our Associate Concertmaster Serge Kardalian, a kind and educated man whom I admired from the beginning. His Ouzo parties after concerts probably damaged some of my memories of that tour, but Serge and I were buddies. Concertmasters Henry Siegl and Karl-Ove

Mannberg shared duties at the time as well, and they also made me feel warmly embraced by the symphony, even as I struggled to keep up.

In 1982, my legs went strangely numb when I received an early morning phone call that Serge had died suddenly of a heart

With Serge Kardalian in Hamburg, Germany, 1980

attack the night before during a recital he was playing in Tacoma. He was 42 years old. Never before had I lost a close friend like that. As a pallbearer along with several other symphony colleagues, I was able to honor him one last time.

It was through this turn of fate that management asked me for the first time ever to fill in as concertmaster for what had been some of Serge's duties. My mind reeled: Concertmaster. Major symphony orchestra. Even as those forlorn years without violin were fading into history, this achievement felt undeserved and incongruous. Only through a tragic default did I find myself suddenly sitting in that principal chair. Sweating buckets at my first rehearsal as concertmaster, I did not feel up to the responsibility. There is no more prominent position in the orchestra, and this time, I nearly toppled over from the vertigo.

13

Even as these years passed, my hands still struggled to keep up with the two or three folders of difficult repertoire required of us each week. I still could not shake the physical

Seattle, 1982

discomfort and technical awkwardness that continued to plague me, and it could not be practiced away. Although my fingers had developed pad-like surfaces, it remained a mystery why, even with all this playing, no hard calluses were returning to my fingertips. I could play to a certain level, but my technique often felt artificial and attempts to play as I dreamed took exhausting effort.

I was walking a fine line. As much as I tried to exhibit a solid violin technique, a distrust of my hands weighed heavily, and the inconsistency of good and bad days, even as assistant concertmaster, shook me profoundly. My success felt unwarranted as I battled with what often felt like a greased bow, and a left hand that still felt wrong. Part of my daily performance at the symphony became simply an attempt to conceal this lingering inadequacy. No one seemed to discern this, except for the occasional commentary on my hilarious bow-grip. *You look so bad but sound so good* was a "compliment" I was to hear more than once. I envied colleagues who played so well and yet so casually, and who invested in fine violins as a matter of course. I envied what seemed to be the luxurious presumption that tomorrow they would still be playing at all.

Trusting this new future with violin had all along felt perilous, as my technique so often seemed poised to crash down into a ball of tendonitis. A precipice loomed that I did not want to go over twice in one lifetime and the extreme anxiety had me heading straight for an early demise.

I struck back preemptively. In a life where the distress of playing the violin so often intertwined itself with the joy of it, I searched for an answer. Opening my eyes to the beauty that surrounded me, I set in motion what is now my saga of life on the sea. In 1986, I moved myself and most that I own aboard a sailboat. The balance was finally struck. The boat offered counterpoise and distraction from the violin, a haven of peace and a place to dream.

The move was filled with meaning, and I could think of only one obvious name with which to christen the boat. In a pact with fate, I swore that should violin ever fail me again, *Poème* and I would disappear over the horizon forever.

Still, driven with a fanatical impulse to reclaim life as a violinist, I could not help but grasp at anything that came my way. Playing in the Seattle Symphony itself opened doors. In 1987, I was invited to join the Mostly Mozart Festival Orchestra in New York City. The festival at Lincoln Center, as well as the orchestra's many tours to Tokyo, put me on some of the world's most famous stages. This was truly lofty, the music glorious, the travel exciting, and the friendships, lifelong.

Manhattan became a second home for seven weeks each summer and a point of departure for numerous performances at the Kennedy Center in Washington D.C., Tan-glewood in Massachusetts, Chicago's Ravinia Festival

Standing fourth from the left, with Mostly Mozart colleagues on the Lincoln Center plaza, 1990

and into Canada as well. A parade of the world's most exquisite soloists graced our performances, and most wonderful of all, no Mozart piano concerto *ever* got old.

After sixteen summers and nearly 500 concerts with Mostly Mozart, it would have been possible to start taking it for granted. Yet throughout the years, I could only bow my head in reverence. How many times, in front of a full house at Avery Fisher Hall, would I close my eyes and transport back to the toy department at Meier & Frank or to my shag-carpeted basement in southeast Portland. My heart could find no answer to the question: How did *that* come to *this*?

14

My tenure with the Seattle Symphony can now be measured in decades, in thousands of pieces of repertoire and in what must amount to billions of notes. At times, it feels like about a billion per week. From gritty and difficult concerts to glorious moments there are no words for, the symphony is where violin and I have tested each other in both love and angry suspicion a thousand times.

Trying to love the violin again came at an exhausting price, but its vibrations of beauty and melody were always the reasons I hoped to live another day. Adding my voice to a Mahler symphony or a Schumann piano concerto would send me home shivering in ecstasy, and this happened hundreds and then thousands of times over the years.

There were also the unexpected glimpses of the celestial. Locking eyes with Emanuel Ax deep in the thunder of Brahms, sharing the heat of Pinchas Zukerman's sweat as he triumphed through Beethoven, even the brush of Itzhak Perlman's tailcoat as he passed by; these were indelible and historic moments of pure enchantment. These were dreams of my youth coming true.

When Yo-Yo Ma and his Silk Road ensemble needed an extra violinist, I had a front row seat to his creative depth. What fortune, that with whoever might be appearing with the Seattle Symphony over the years, the fleeting moments together at the mountain top always rewarded me with a secret bond with them:

Yo-Yo Ma

that of suspending time together through music, dazzled together under the same spell.

Performing as concertmaster on many occasions humbly placed me on intimate musical terms with some of the world's finest musicians. It is seductive enough just to breathe the same air, but when Renee Fleming came to town and performed Strauss's duet *Morgen* with solo violin, I believe the earth did move. Along with me, the audience was probably levitating throughout Ms. Fleming's performance. Her encore of Strauss's *Caecilie* brought the house down.

The earth seemed to shift again as Mstislav Rostropovitch conducted his last concerts in Seattle. The violin solos in Shostakovitch's first symphony – melodies a violinist can only dream of – hopefully sang from my violin as tearfully as I felt them. Every moment of the Shostakovitch seemed to mean something personal to Rostropovitch. I couldn't help but pose a rather obvious question during a rehearsal break: "Could Shostakovitch really have been aware of how profoundly beautiful

Mstislav Rostropovirch

his own melodies were?" Having been a close colleague and friend of Shostakovitch years ago, Rostropovitch leaned forward with thoughtful sincerity. With a hand on mine, he assured me that aching beauty resided deep within Shostakovitch, and he knew exactly how to express it through music.

Rostropovitch was little more than a year from the end of his life. It was his recording of the Dvorak concerto that my family grew up listening to during the years my brother studied cello. To embrace him now was my chance to honor our greatest family hero of so many years ago.

What more fortune could then possibly come my way than to appear as Marvin Hamlisch's concertmaster and straight-man for his years of Pops concerts in Seattle. Laughter and great music made every evening a precious memory. Violin solos at the Pops, always soulful and stylistic, were where I sang my sweetest, and Marvin always made it easy for me.

Whether the theme was Broadway music, movie scores, Christmas favorites, or Cole Porter, many of us felt a transcendence when Marvin arrived for a week of Pops. The audiences certainly felt the same. For me though, a confusion persisted. I came to know well his voice, his moods, his expressions, his humor, and especially the back of his head as he sat at the piano. But what I could never fully grasp, was finding myself even this close to this particular man of artistry and renown. The unlikely chance of that happening was the most impossible of all.

Marvin Hamlisch

15

Most of a lifetime has passed now since that summer of 1971, the summer Elaine Richey showed me the moon. By my own standards, I never was able to put Humpty-Dumpty back together again. Any measure of success I achieved with the violin was but the crawl back from oblivion. I wondered if returning to the violin was even a fair endeavor, as my hands never again equaled what they were at age seventeen.

A sense of guilt at having re-entered the music world under pretense plagued me all my decades of symphony life, as such a huge chunk of me had died so long ago. I never came close to graduating from music conservatory or completing a musical education. The study of music history and theory and of the evolution of styles and influences of composers never interested me. The subjects, as vital an as intriguing as they are, reeked trite and irrelevant to my very soul if I could not play the violin to begin with. Some colleagues have probably sensed this gaping void with a degree of consternation as, to this day, I would just as soon discuss philosophy or diesel mechanics. Violin and life itself took on a deep melancholy that never left, as well as a dark suspicion that all hangs by a thread. It was only the memory and power of what had been that seemed to pull me through.

It was about more than just a career or rubbing elbows with famous people. The vibration of playing the violin was the point for me; playing with it, toying with it, exalting and singing through it, crying through it. That was the point, and where the line between spiritual life and death felt drawn. Along with the Mozart *Requiem*, a Rachmaninoff piano concerto or a Brahms symphony, it was the violin vibrating through me that made life worth living.

There was great benefit in facing such a fall so early in life. It forced changes in the very fiber by which I viewed existence. Unwillingly compelled to grow and strengthen down a different path, my real education began when forced to approach life's questions with the deepest skepticism.

I lost all my arguments with reality as I cursed fate for robbing me of what I considered to be my rightful destiny, my sense of permanence, and for destroying every last ounce of my courage. Especially at a young age when time moved slowly, and when what was supposed to be a glorious future lay in ruin. From the bottom of my soul I cursed fate, even though I had only myself to blame.

Intellectual dishonesty got me nowhere as I struggled to find my place in the world. The repercussions of my trauma with violin color my perspective to this day, on what is true in life and what is fantasy. With this more somber perspective I still wonder: if this defining event had not occurred, if my vertical path with violin had instead continued to fruition, in what other musical cosmos might I find myself today.

About two decades after leaving Indiana University, I was fortunate to meet Ruggiero Ricci one final time. He had come to Seattle to play Bruch's *Scottish Fantasy* with us at the Seattle Center Opera House. I felt compelled to attempt a connection with him, but this time hopefully on a more positive level. I braced myself as I walked to his dressing room, and can recall my exact words to him: *I hope you don't remember me because I was your worst student!* He laughed so hard and hugged me so tight, I couldn't tell if he really remembered me or not. But it was a wonderful moment, and suddenly some of the pain from IU that had weighed in my heart for so long . . . simply vanished.

I often return to the windows of my old basement apartment in Portland, and also to the spot I last saw my Greek Goddess in the department store. I still visit these places, to contemplate the years I lived without the violin, to reflect on and honor somehow the saddest days of my life.

It was never lost on me that I had been reborn. And that I could not have been more fortunate for the chance to reclaim a life in music; for the chance to cross paths with all my heroes, and most especially for the unlikely chance that the passion between violin and me had not been lost forever. I do wonder, though, whether something deeper may have entered my playing along the way. A powerful sensation endures, that each note, each phrase and every nuance of vibrato still feels pulled out of those years, even so long ago, of despair.

It seems only yesterday that Elaine Richey was demonstrating her liquid bow changes, her sensuous vibrato and her silken tone. Imparting her love and mastery of the violin. I still try to honor her with every note I play.

As long as I continue to take my place on stage with the symphony, audiences may behold a graying violinist embracing yet another moment in the sun. Inside my heart though, and between the violin and me, I'm seventeen years old. No one is more grateful for such a life in music, but what I wouldn't give to turn back the clock.

AFTERWORD

Elaine Richey enriched the lives of her many violin students wherever she taught. While based in North Carolina, she spent her summers playing and teaching in Sun Valley, Sugar Mountain, Snowbird and Taos. Her popularity grew to over-whelming proportions as one of the country's most sought after pedagogues. Violinists flocked to her in droves in her final years as she taught at the Saugatuck Music Festival in Michigan. She died of pancreatic cancer in 1997 at age 65.

Tom Raimondi and I remained close friends for many years. Although it

Elaine Richey

Tom Raimondi

sounded mysterious to me, he claimed a holistic ability to heal various maladies and eventually conducted seminars around the country teaching his "Raimondi Technique". While passing through Seattle on business he would be sure to call for a visit, as we always had plenty to reminisce about and celebrate. His visits mysteriously and abruptly ended about ten years ago, which began to worry me greatly. My best investigative efforts lead me to accept that he passed away without my knowledge in 2005.

I believe that without Tom's faith in me, or our meeting by utter chance at Portland State, I would never have played the violin again.

In the summer of 2002, almost thirty years after leaving Indiana University, I revisited the campus to explore my memories of the place. High on my list of priorities was to inquire about my astronomy professor, Dr. Frank Edmondson.

Professor Edmondson

After some detective work I found him, cane in hand, ambling down the path near Swain West. He could not possibly remember me, but his face lit with joy as I gushed my gratitude for his lectures so long ago. He was within his final years of life, and I bowed my head upon reading of his passing in 2008 at age 96.

Sally, left, and I at Camden School for girls

Sally Beamish 2012

Sally Beamish, the pen pal I made at the Camden School for Girls while touring England with the Portland Junior Symphony in 1970, grew up and became the well-known classical composer. After attending a performance of her work in San Francisco, Sally made her way to Seattle in 2012. We had a delightful reunion and a chance to review together the last forty-two years of our lives.

My cousin Thomas Schmidt continued on his path as a concert pianist, performing and touring for years as a founding member of the renowned Arden Piano Trio. Today, he is the organist and choral director at St. Peters Church in New York City. He lives with his wife, Kathy, in Harlem.

Carol continued her love of ballet and for six years danced with the Portland Ballet Company. She later moved to New York City where she married Jonathan Segal, an eloquent jazz pianist and music educator, and raised a family. To this day, she runs her clients through exercise regimens as a "hard body" personal trainer.

Paul was always a finer musician than I. After his years with cello, academics and a stint in the army, he was struck down by severe clinical schizophrenia. He is the only schizophrenic I know who could quote Faulkner and perform a perfect ricochet bowing. Today he lives in Portland under care and medications. But he recalls with clarity and humor our early years of ballet and music-making.

Mom taught ethnic dance and vocal music in the Portland Public Schools for more than twenty years. She devoted the last decades of her life to Paul's welfare and became active with the National Alliance on Mental Illness (NAMI) for support and guidance. She lived a simple life alone for years after retirement, and died in 2012. Her ashes lie buried under her favorite tree.

Dad was a church organist and choral director for almost forty years. After retirement he continued to teach music at the Montessori Earth School in Portland, and fully wrote three childrens operas for performances there. *Speak to the Earth, From the Wilderness* and *Children of the Island* are Dad's admonitions to the young to embrace humanity and care for their planet. Concerned on a political level for the ecology of local fishing lakes in Oregon, he still fantasizes about getting a line in the water. He takes raising his annual crop of tomatoes very seriously, since he turned 91 in 2013. Dad lives one day at a time, does his crosswords, and threatens to outlive us all.

During the last decade of Mom's life, things turned tender again between Mom and Dad. Carol and I often returned home to Portland for holidays, and after picking up Paul, we would gather as a family of five to remember our lives together, to laugh and sing around the table once more.

Marvin Hamlisch

For a period of nearly seven years, Marvin Hamlisch delighted Seattle Pops audiences with his unique combination of musical genius and droll humor.

After meeting for about the fiftieth time, no words could have sounded sweeter than his grunt "You again?" He had a high voice for a man his size, and everything he said sounded like it was off the cuff and clipped, like an afterthought or one-liner.

Marvin ran through rehearsals quickly and would sometimes snap in anger when things went wrong:

"Trombones, you missed your entrance!"

"We don't even have the sheet music for this piece in our folder!" was the reply.

Marvin's tantrums were short-lived. He would gush an apology, make some self-deprecating wisecrack, and with a wave of his hand, squeak out a girlish giggle. Hard not to forgive.

At concerts, I would always precede Marvin onstage to get the orchestra tuned just before his own entrance. I think he had a stock supply of his own send-offs. Traditionally, it's "break a leg", but not so with Marvin. With earthshaking emotion in his voice, he would bolster my courage as the stage door opened for me: "I want you to go out there and tune that orchestra like you've *never* tuned before!" Since tuning an orchestra requires nothing more than a nod to the principal oboist, I would nearly trip while laughing my way onto the stage.

In 2009, I worried that a preplanned skit with Marvin had gone a little too far. For a Pops series featuring Sha-Na-Na, the orchestra was invited to dress up 1950's style with whatever we could put together, but Marvin appeared onstage in his usual set of tails. As he turned to the audience after the overture, I charged from my seat, as per our sketch to interrupt his opening remarks:

Marvin Hamlisch

"Excuse me! . . . Marvin! . . . didn't you get the memo?!
Many of us went to some trouble to dress for the mood of this concert,
but apparently you felt this was too much bother?
It didn't occur to you to make a little effort?
It's all a little upsetting and . . . well there, that's how I feel,
now you know! "

As I skulked back to my chair, Marvin stood there a little more stunned than I expected:

"The last time I was scolded like that was by someone in my own family!"

Concerned that I may have truly upset him, I asked at intermission if my acting had been too realistic, but he said, " No, keep it coming!"

Marvin was passionate to the end and not surprisingly spent part of each Pops concert encouraging the youngsters in the audience to make this timeless music part of their lives forever.

August 2012

At approximately 24 degrees north latitude and 157 degrees west longitude, in the middle of the Pacific ocean, I was playing some Bach for the sailing crew of Kotuku. I doubted very much that Bach had ever been played at those coordinates before. The five of us aboard were sailing the 39-foot sloop back to Seattle from Hawaii, a spectacular journey across an infinitely majestic ocean. Our days were filled with rotating three-hour watches, sunsets, porpoises, whales and the occasional somber albatross.

Each day was an adventure, but I was also looking forward to getting home to begin a new season with the symphony. Kotuku was about 750 nautical miles north of Oahu when the sea and sky suddenly seemed to take on a darker and more ominous beauty. We had received an email by marine radio that sat me down cold.

What a place to be, to learn that Marvin had died. There was nothing to be done but hold on tight to the memories that flooded back and that I will cherish forever. In that personal moment I imagined performing "I Could Have Danced All Night", rhapsodizing with him once again in a dim spotlight, fading now to black.

Japan

In 1988, I began studying Japanese obsessively, and three years later took a year's leave from the Seattle Symphony to seek adventure and fortune in a foreign land. Through chance friendships, I was invited to audition for the Nagoya Symphony. It was an interesting process in which the violin players themselves vote on candidates. They took a chance on me, and I ended up playing about half of the season with them. Rehearsals playing the violin are difficult enough, but rehearsals conducted in Japanese added a great deal of humor to my musical life in Nagoya.

With ladies of the Nagoya Symphony, 1992

I became fairly confident in conversational Japanese, but my skills were sometimes tested while under duress. My daily routine with the Nagoya Symphony began with a bus ride from Bisai City to Owari-Ichinomiya, followed by a train ride into Nagoya, and finally a subway ride to wherever it was we were rehearsing or performing. I used *kaisuuken*, booklets of discount tickets for the bus and train, but I used cash for the subway. One day, I arrived at Nagoya Station to discover I had forgotten my wallet. I had only enough change for about half a subway fare, so I had to think quickly. My Japanese flowed quite beautifully, I thought, as I pleaded with the ticket agent to rescue me: *Onegai shimasu, tasukete kudasai! Saifu o wasuremashita!* (I beg you, rescue me! I forgot my wallet!) Wearing a suit with a violin strapped on my back probably helped convince him I was "indispensable" for the upcoming concert. He slid a free ticket under the window.

In order to obtain a work-permit for the Nagoya Symphony, I had to leave Japan and file through an embassy or consulate. The island of Guam was a reasonable choice, and sounded exotic enough, so I found myself on an American Airlines four-day holiday package along with many smoking businessmen and giggling newlyweds. Obtaining the work visa was effortless. But on that Thanksgiving week in 1991, Guam suffered its most destructive typhoon in ten years. The eye of super-typhoon Yuri came within 50 miles of Guam, and by mid-afternoon, the wind gusts felt like a solid mass.

After dinner, I huddled in my hotel room where I stayed glued to the radio as the hurricane gathered strength and peaked around 9:30 that Wednesday night. It was an odd opportunity to study the layout of the island, as radio reports of damage came in from all corners. By Thursday morning, the sky and ocean were only slightly unsettled, but all the palm trees had been brutally stripped of their branches.

In 1997, I flew to Akita, Japan, a special lady-friend's home town. I had asked her to find an amateur pianist in the area capable of accompanying me so I could play several easy pieces for her folks and a few friends. No big deal, I thought. Instead, she found a piano professor from the local college who in turn arranged something much more than I was prepared for. I was driven to a small music school where, as the hour approached, an audience began arriving by the car-full. Nearly a hundred children with their parents filled the hall to capacity as I glared in shock at my friend: *"What the #&%$???"* It was stifling hot. I was in sandals and jeans, sweating and unrehearsed, but I had no choice. I launched into what became a recital with the lovely pianist. In my best Japanese, I explained that this was just going to be an evening of "violin play" and nothing formal: "Please, simply enjoy the sound of a violin," I said.

We played one short piece after another: *Cavatina, Cantabile, Meditation from Thaïs, Beau Soir, Allegro Brillante, Banjo and Fiddle, Valse Bluette,* and some Corelli.

After about an hour of music and my mostly comedic Japanese commentary, I wasn't sure how it was going over as the applause seemed formal and controlled. Convinced I had outstayed my welcome, I thanked them for coming and announced that the recital was over, but no one moved. An awkward silence fell on the room until from the back of the hall a child's gentle voice spoke one word: *"An-ko-ru!"*. "Encore". To a burst of applause, we played Raff's *Cavatina* once more and I felt I had won the hearts of those kind people.

I traveled throughout Japan and home-stayed with a wonderful family in Gifu Prefecture for several months. Grandma Hanako was 88 years old and walked arm in arm with me outside among the crops. She told of running for her life near the Nagaragawa River while the city of Gifu was bombed during World War II. While I lived as a member of the Asano family, I taught English alongside their daughter Yoko at various locations in the area.

One of the classrooms where young students gathered for English class happened to be within the walls of a small music academy in Bisai City. The academy's owner, Junko Iwata, had three extremely talented young daughters. It was a match made in heaven. In return for living rent-free in an apartment within the Mozart Music Academy, I gave the owner's eight year old daughter, Nanae, violin lessons. Over time I became deeply involved with yet another Japanese family.

With Nanae in the Mozart Music Academy

I was inspired by Iwata-san. She did not want her girls to suffer along demurely in her own footsteps. During a drive together on errands, Iwata-san pulled to the curb and turned off the engine. She turned to plead that, in the event of her own demise, would I take Nanae to America for all the opportunities she would find there. Mom is still alive and well, but in the ensuing years Nanae did move to the United States, graduate from Juilliard, and marry a fine cellist who is a recent addition to the New York Philharmonic. Nanae's invitation to attend her wedding in Brooklyn meant the world to me. At the reception, her father thanked me for opening the door for her, but I could only be eternally grateful in return.

A most tender evening in Japan had as its beginning a chance meeting in New York City. At times during my summers with Mostly Mozart, I would spend an afternoon at the South Street Seaport in lower Manhattan where the imposing historic barque *Peking* is moored. Tugging at her lines behind the *Peking* is a much smaller sailing vessel, the 100 year old schooner *Pioneer*, which takes groups out for sails in the harbor. Ticket in hand, I stepped aboard the *Pioneer* and met Yurie, a uniquely stunning young Japanese woman who was working as crew.

During the two hour sail, I gained her trust and a friendship ensued. Hearing of my upcoming Mostly Mozart tour to Tokyo, she urged me to visit her mother and sister in Toyama if I could get myself there. After our concerts in Tokyo that summer, I stayed in Japan and made a point of doing just that.

Arriving by train in Toyama, I was greeted by Yurie's sister who drove me to the family house. As is usual Japanese custom, it seemed the whole neighborhood turned out for an evening of food and frivolity. The younger crowd tried to correct my textbook Japanese into their own dialect, and my attempts sent them reeling with laughter.

The following day, Yurie's Mother, sister and I drove an hour into the countryside to visit the grandparents and other relatives. No one spoke English there and I had to swim a bit trying to keep up with the conversation. In the evening, we enjoyed dinner in the Japanese tradition on tatami matting, and afterward I attempted to serenade the group with a slow melody. The music seemed to accompany the mood of the darkening sky, and some of the relatives wiped tears away as one by one I greeted them around the table. The old grandpa took my hand finally and in simple Japanese almost cried into my eyes: "From the bottom of my heart I am so happy to meet you". He had been in the Japanese Navy during World War II and had never before met an American.

Radio Friends

My youthful obsession with radios took another turn after moving to Seattle. With so many early days of uncertainty with the violin, learning Morse code and receiving an amateur radio license provided yet more balance and distraction. My log over the years shows several hundred contacts world-wide with code alone, but eventually voice communication became the obvious choice. Radio communications are a boater's link to civilization ashore, so this old hobby retained its thrill and came in very useful later in life.

An entire ham-radio community exists in the air around us, and among the more local "2-meter" enthusiasts, friendships are easily made. All the hams address each other on a first name and call-sign basis. Over time, I became familiar with some of these faceless voices.

After a Pops concert years ago, I was informed that there were visitors for me in the Green Room, but when I entered saw no one that I knew. "John? Hi, I'm Bob, W7JVE!" His voice sounded like that of an old friend. Bob and his wife, Joann, were longtime Pops fans, and for years afterward, I would be sure to give them a personal bow from the stage. Bob and Joann were active as models, character actors in local television commercials and as movie extras over the years. We became lifetime friends, and I had a sad honor to speak at Bob's memorial service in 2009. Joann and I still keep in touch, and she still gets her own bow at the Pops.

Poème

Loving the violin again saved my life. But having a boat in my life saved me from the violin. For more than two-and-a-half decades, I have greeted each day from aboard the sailboat. It has always provided safe haven, comfort and adventure. The boat also provided a specific diversion so that my ordeal with the violin did not defeat me. Life on a boat is a life on the edge. It is not settled in one place, it's built for exploration and adventure, and it's attuned to the basic rhythms of the earth and sea. As incongruous as a boat-life may seem with the life of a classical violinist, in fact the dangers and uncertainties seem to have paralleled each other in my case. The perils seem normal now, the style unique, and the life an enchanted one.

Across Puget Sound, the mountains look stunning, and if I'm lucky, a bald eagle is presiding over the marina from atop the breakwater. With my violin slung over my shoulder, I step off the boat for the long walk down the dock while mentally going down my list:

". . . music, keys, wallet . . . bilge is dry." The day is going to be a little rough at the symphony rehearsal – some complex contemporary work followed by a demanding Mendelssohn symphony – so I hold onto what I can of the moment's serenity.

It's about a 20-minute drive to the concert hall. I keep my tails and tuxedo in a locker there since they would take up too much space on the boat. By the time I get to the hall, I am already warmed up on the violin because I ran up and down the fingerboard beforehand aboard the boat. After grabbing a cup of coffee and checking some last-minute fingerings, I'm seated on stage with my colleagues for the first downbeat of the rehearsal. The music takes all my concentration, but midstream in the slow movement of the Mendelssohn my mind wanders back to the boat: "Do my zincs need changing?" By about 4 p.m. we finish our second rehearsal of the day, and it's time to head home to the ocean air.

There is likely a boat project waiting that I cannot put off any longer. Staying afloat and not catching fire are the two overriding principles of successful boat ownership, but the list of maintenance and installation projects is as endless as any house.

Experimenting in the galley for friends and dining in the salt air of a unique Seattle ambiance while music wafts from the speakers has always felt like the perfect evening. Over time, I found that the best things in life seem to come together on a boat. Arriving home after a concert or opera in the dark of night and walking to the far end of a long dock may seem anti-climactic. But the thrill of the concert remains, the music still reverbarating harmoniously with my return.

Still in full effect is my pact with fate, where at any time the horizon may beckon me forever. In fact I have chased that horizon many times with the boat, but so far only to peek over the edge. Whether during a quick sail to Port Madison on Bainbridge Island, or to an anchorage off Poulsbo, the wind in the sails became my therapy of choice. Special outings include sailing in tandem with other boats, then rafting together at anchor to toast the sunset. Across the treacherous Strait of Juan de Fuca, the San Juan Islands and the Gulf Islands of Canada have become almost annual destinations.

To wherever I may drop the anchor, I take my entire home with me. And to wherever I may sail, the violin comes along as well. Whether for some gentle Bach at raft-ups or impromptu recitals at pubs and homes along the way, my violin is always part of the picture.

The love of my life is never far from my reach.

Acknowledgements

I am very grateful to the friends and professionals who helped bring this book to fruition. Editing out my grammatical errors had to be a nightmare for Charles Gates of New York City. Encouraging me along the way was my sister Carol Segal, symphony cellist and sailing cohort Walter Gray, violinist Tim Garland, Canadian pals Tommy Tompkins and Michele Hall, and Dan Barton, an educator who lives a few boats away down the dock. Giving me heartfelt and invaluable feedback on the text were Steve Odom, Rosemary Odom, Vicki Jacobson, Ella Gray and Josie Solseng. I am especially grateful to my longtime colleague and friend Ira Lieberman who offered the Foreword as well as his timeless counsel. Finally, guiding and protecting me from the beginning of the process was my lady Yoshiko Imoto. For her caring and maturity, I have a better book. For her love and wisdom, I am a better person.

Photo Captions

1) Young string quartet, 1968: John, Paul, Randy Kelly, now principal violist of the Pittsburgh Symphony, and Regan Crowley, now violinist with the BBC Symphony Orchestra in London

2) Dad gave me a soldering iron as a gift upon my Confirmation at St. Michael's.

3) Weller family, 1959, with foster sister Beverly (standing)

4) Dad, Paul and John at Lake James, Indiana, 1977

5) Playing for Mom and nephew Noah, Portland, 1984

6) Sun Valley Music Camp, Dollar Cabin, 1969. We watched the moon landing from this room.

7) Portland Junior Symphony program, 1966

8) Family reunion, Portland, 1983

9) "Fiddler on the Roof", Friday Harbor, Washington

10) Hiroshima, 1992

11) With Dad at Silver Lake, Washington c. 1985

12) With Pinchas Zuckerman on Mostly Mozart tour to upstate New York and Canada.

13) Aboard the sailboat "Quest" with Yoshiko and friends in Friday Harbor, Washington, 2002. This is the very boat hijacked by Somali pirates in 2011, where all four Americans aboard were killed, including owner Scott Adam, at left.

14) Mozart Music Academy, Bisai-City, Japan, 1992

15) A gift from Eugene Fodor

16) With Dad, Lake James, Indiana, 2007

17) With Doc Severinsen, 2009

18) Aboard Poeme

19) Playing string quartets in the Grand Canyon! 2008

20) With Mom, 2010

21) Warming up backstage, 2012. Emanuel Ax is at the piano preparing to rehearse Brahms' 2nd piano concerto.

22) Concertmaster for the "James Bond" Pops series, 2012

23) Ferry get-away to Bainbridge Island

24) Practicing aboard Poeme

25) At the helm of Kotuku, Pacific Ocean, 2012. Photo by Steve Odom

26) At the dock in Poulsbo

Poème is a Taiwan-built 36-foot cutter-rigged Lord Nelson sailboat. The hull is heavily built of fiberglass, with teak decks and a 40 horsepower Yanmar diesel engine. The interior is constructed of teak, oriental ash and rosewood. Poème weighs about 14 tons and is designed for ocean sailing.